Praise for

Mary and the Interior Life

"The relationship between a son and his mother can be among the most intimate and tender of human relationships. (Blessed are the sons and mothers who know the truth of this from their own experience!) Fr. Jeremiah gives his readers a generous invitation into his own rich and beautiful relationship with our Blessed Mother in his new book *Mary and the Interior Life*. The reader who responds to his invitation and follows his lead will be blessed deeply—even eternally so."

—Mother Clare Matthiass, CFR,
author of *Discerning Religious Life* and *The Light in You*

"Fr. Jeremiah Shryock, CFR, has written a truly beautiful book. Frankly, it is a must-read for everyone aspiring to enter more deeply into the life of holiness and Mary's role in leading souls to a total self-offering and surrender to God. Inspired passages and uniquely contemplative insights fill the pages of this book as Fr. Jeremiah ponders the mysteries of the Rosary and Mary's presence in the Gospel accounts with a great heart of love. Fr. Jeremiah calls himself now a Marian hermit taught by Mary; clearly, he has been a very fine student and son in placing himself receptively before the profound instructions of his Virgin Mother."

—Fr. Donald Haggerty,
author of *St. John of the Cross: Master of Contemplation*,
The Contemplative Hunger, Contemplative Provocations

"I prayed my way through this book. Each chapter holds many things to marvel at and pray with—to ponder, in imitation of Mary herself. Father Jeremiah's spiritual fatherhood is at its best as he reveals to us the glories of the Mother of Our Lord and invites us to learn from her what he has learned through years of deep prayer and conversation with her and her Son: that we were made for nothing less than divine intimacy, interior freedom, and radical, self-giving love."

—**Claire Dwyer,**
author, *This Present Paradise: A Spiritual Journey with St. Elizabeth of the Trinity*

"All saints have a devotion to Mary. If you desire to be a saint and have yet to find a way to join with her in your pilgrimage into the heart of God, Fr. Jeremiah will show you the way."

—**Dan Burke,**
Avila Institute for Spiritual Formation

"Profound insights drawn from a life lived in union with Mary is what you would expect to find in a book written by a Franciscan priest living as a Marian hermit. In *Mary and the Interior Life*, Fr. Jeremiah Myriam Shryock does not disappoint. It's a great book and will inspire you to fall more in love with Jesus, Mary, and the mysteries of salvation."

—**Fr. Donald Calloway, MIC,**
Vicar Provincial, Marian Fathers

Mary
and the
Interior Life

Jeremiah Myriam Shryock, CFR

PARACLETE PRESS
Brewster, Massachusetts

2023 First Printing

Mary and the Interior Life

Copyright © 2023 by The Community of the Franciscan Friars of the Renewal

ISBN 978-1-64060-914-3

Library of Congress Control Number: 2023942421

10 9 8 7 6 5 4 3 2 1

Front cover image: *The Annunciation* by Henry Ossawa Tanner
Used with permission of the Philadelphia Museum of Art: Purchased with the W. P. Wilstach Fund, 1899, W1899-1-1

Published by Paraclete Press
Brewster, Massachusetts
www.paracletepress.com

Printed in the United States of America

I dedicate this book to
the Monastic family of Bethlehem
in Livingston Manor, New York,

whose vocation, and generosity to me, have not
only enabled me to write this book but, more
importantly, have helped me to live the mystery of
Mary's interior life more deeply. Their vocation is a
treasured gift to the Church. I am eternally grateful
to each one of them.

Contents

Foreword

When we read the Gospel of John, Christian hearts spontaneously realize that what the Lord Jesus said to Nicodemus, to the woman at the well, to the man born blind, to Martha and Mary of Bethany, and to many others, Jesus is in fact saying to each one and all of us. So, too, it is when Jesus spoke to his beloved disciple who was standing with Mary the mother of the Lord near the cross. Jesus said to his beloved disciple: *"Behold, your mother"* (John 19:27). In that moment, Jesus was not speaking exclusively to that one disciple and was not simply making housing arrangements for his mother. Rather, Jesus was speaking to us all, and revealing to us a crucial saving truth. God has given us Mary to be our spiritual mother. From that hour, in obedience to the Lord Jesus, the beloved disciple *"took her to his own home"* (John 19:27). Technically, in the original Greek, it does not say he took her into his home or house. It says he took her into "his own" (*ta idia*). It means he took her into his heart. The beloved disciple's act of doing so was an essential lesson about what it means to be a disciple of Jesus. To be a disciple of the Lord Jesus is, among other things, to take Mary the mother of Jesus into our own hearts and to abandon all to her presence, her love, and her care. She has received from the Lord the mission, and therefore the grace, to be a mother to us all. *"Woman, behold, your son"* (John 19:26).

Just as Mary was the mother of Jesus and worked to raise him and form him, so similarly Mary is the spiritual mother of you and me and works to raise us and form us by grace. From her place now on high in the heavenly places, she devotes herself to certain works of spiritual maternity. She prays for us, she protects us, she leads us, and she is always there for us with an abundance of compassion every step of the way. She knows well that our walk is with Christ, and that the purpose of following Christ is to become another Christ. Yet, she also knows how our walk with Christ involves many others in Christ—with our fellow Christians on earth, with the saints in heaven, with the angels too, and especially with her. Her place in the grand scheme of things is to work in a maternal way in our lives until each of us grows by grace *"to the measure of the stature of the fullness of Christ" (Ephesians 4:13).*

Down through the centuries of the Church, the Spirit has gradually brought to light from out of the Scriptures the truth and the mystery of Mary. Who is this woman? How should we relate to her? The Word and the Spirit have taught us not only that she is the Mother of God but also the Mother of the Church. Indeed, Mary is for each of us our own personal spiritual mother. You and I are called to respond to the gift God has given to us in her, and the great question is how. How, practically speaking, should you and I respond to the woman whom God has appointed to be the spiritual mother of us all?

One of the most ancient hymns to Mary, the *Sub tuum*, has been found on a papyrus fragment in Egypt dated to the mid-second century after Christ. The hymn itself is likely older than the fragment, and perhaps goes back to some of the earliest Christians. It shows how they responded to Mary. The hymn goes like this: *"To you do we come seeking mercy, O Mother of Christ our God. Do not turn away, nor despise our prayer, but be pleased to hear our plea. Entreat your Son, our God, to save our souls."* The hymn reveals a certain confidence in Mary. It also offers a petition to her. It is a response to Mary born from the grace of a living relationship with her, but a relationship directed to greater union with her Son Jesus Christ.

All of the sound developments in devotion to Mary down through the centuries are but an expansion of the same grace revealed in this prayer—the grace of a relationship with Mary that is all about Jesus.

It is difficult to put into words the nature of our relationship with Mary. To explain it well is challenging even for the greatest saints and mystics. On the one hand, it is a relationship with Mary. On the other hand, it is all about Jesus. If one talks too much about Mary, the relationship seems to be all about Mary, but it is not. If one talks only about Jesus, there seems to be no relationship with Mary, but there is. It is hard to do justice to the mystery of a profound relationship with her that is altogether about him. It is even more challenging to proclaim to the Christian people the possibility of a union of hearts with Mary by grace, and to do so in such a way that people can really receive that grace, enter into the mystery of it, and spiritually profit from it. However, Father Jeremiah Shryock has done it. *Mary and the Interior Life* is a book that tells a saving truth. It tells of a profound love for Mary, and it points out the way to living in a union of hearts with her, but a love-union with her that is all about Jesus.

God calls preachers to bear witness to the truth, but there are many ways to do so. Father Jeremiah's way is personal, testimonial, scriptural, and practical. He speaks from his own experience, yet in terms drawn from the Scripture and the tradition of the Church. He offers innumerable examples and lessons from his own life and relationship with Mary, but the point is to announce that you and I can live the mystery too. What he proposes is not novel. Saints Louis de Montfort, Maximilian Kolbe, John Paul II, and Mother Teresa of Calcutta have already gone down the road of living in close personal union with Mary. Father Jeremiah has simply taken them seriously and followed in their footsteps. What is so helpful and compelling in his account of living the interior life with Mary is the real-life quality of the whole thing. Speaking from his own Christian walk and vivid relationship with Mary, Father Jeremiah tells the mysteries of her life as lessons for our own in how to follow Christ. Mary figures prominently in the story, but the story is all about following Jesus.

The story is important because following Jesus Christ on the pathways of discipleship should normally lead by grace to becoming a contemplative soul. Contemplative souls are people who are aware of the Presence of God living in their hearts by grace and shining out all around us in nature. Better still, a contemplative soul is someone who abides in the awareness of the Presence of God and remains responsive to his Presence with a heart full of love. It is high time for Christians to realize that all the baptized are called to become contemplative souls, and the whole Church on earth is called to become the contemplative Church. Scripture says so when Saint Paul asks insistently: *"Do you not know that you are God's temple and that God's Spirit of God dwells in you?" (1 Corinthians 3:16).*

To abide in the loving awareness of Jesus and respond fully to his love, however, is a challenging thing. *"The spirit indeed is willing, but the flesh is weak" (Mark 14:38).* In addition to our personal tendencies to distraction and to sin, the circumstances of the world around us seem to conspire increasingly more against the flourishing of contemplative prayer in our hearts. Indeed, it seems that the world is becoming ever more organized against the very roots of contemplation: faith, silence, prayer. The opposition seems to grow with every passing day. Yet, the Virgin is greater than all the opposition. Her help in the spiritual life is immense—more powerful than anyone could imagine. Given the state of the world today, in order for the Christians to become contemplative souls, in order for us to become the contemplative Church on earth, there is need now for a deeper recourse to the Virgin. What kind of deeper recourse? Father Jeremiah knows, and he tells us the answer in *Mary and the Interior Life.*

—Fr. James Dominic Brent, OP
Dominican House of Studies, Washington, DC

Introduction

July 1, 2021, is a day I will never forget as long as I live. It is the day I became a hermit. For at least five years prior to that, I had been longing to live a more contemplative life. It is a grace, I believe, that God gave me. Becoming a hermit was not something I planned twenty years ago when I entered a very active Franciscan community, nor did I wake up one morning and think, *"I'm going to become a hermit."* Rather, the realization of this grace occurred gradually over the years, as I was drawn to spend longer periods of time in solitude, silence, and prayer.

One of the places where this deepening occurred is at the Monastery of Bethlehem in Livingston Manor, New York. The monastery contains 1,400 acres of woods and is nicely tucked away in the Catskill Mountains. The nuns there live a deeply monastic life that contains both solitude and communal liturgical prayer. After serving the nuns there by celebrating Mass over the years, I was asked by the superior one day if I would consider being their chaplain. She told me that as their chaplain I would live in a hermitage on their property, and the only requirement was that I would celebrate Mass each morning and hear confessions for retreatants. Other than that, the rest of my day would be spent in solitude, silence, and prayer. Without hesitation I replied, "Yes! However, I need permission from my community first."

A few months later, I was granted permission, and my drive to the monastery that morning in July was filled with joy and fascination. "I can't believe this is finally happening," I said to myself. As I pulled into the monastery and parked my car next to the hermitage I would be living in, I asked myself a very important question, "Now what do I do?" The Code of Canon Law states that hermits devote *"their life to the praise of God and the salvation of the world through a stricter withdrawal from the world, the silence of solitude, and assiduous prayer and penance.*[1] These words resounded deeply within my own heart when I first read them, as they still do today. However, my question remained: how do I do that, practically? After all, hermits are like endangered species. I have known many cloistered monks and nuns throughout my life; however, I have never met or known a hermit. Even though I am blessed to have a very wise and holy spiritual director, there was no hermit I knew whom I could call when solitude and silence became difficult.

I walked into my hermitage, and staring directly at me was an icon of Mary, the Mother of God. Immediately, when my eyes met hers, I dropped to my knees and uttered a prayer to her in this fashion: "Mary, I don't know how to be a hermit, but I believe your Son has called me here. Please teach me everything. I have nobody but you to help me." I didn't feel anything spectacular after I prayed that prayer, but within a few days I noticed that something was changing within me. I began to feel more drawn to Mary's presence, to speak with her more regularly and to meditate upon her life, especially in the Scriptures.

On one level, I was already doing this. I had prayed the Rosary every day for twenty years prior to this, and I had always sought her intercession and guidance in my relationship with God. She was, as I will describe more in detail in this book, very influential in my own conversion. However, this was different. It was as if she were taking me by the hand and leading me to places I could never have gone were she not with me, guiding every step of the way. Before I became a hermit, I felt like Mary was always next to me. However, once I moved into the hermitage, I felt like Mary was seated in front of me, teaching me everything.

Recently a retreatant here at the monastery asked me what kind of hermit I was. Without thinking I simply replied, "A Marian hermit."

"A Marian hermit?" the person responded. "What is that? I never heard of that kind of hermit." "Neither have I," I said, "but it means that Mary teaches me everything."

What Mary was teaching me I began to write down in a series of talks that would eventually become a retreat entitled "Mary and the Interior Life." The retreat contained fourteen talks, based upon the fourteen biblical moments of Mary's life. Each talk contained a theme or disposition that is necessary for our spiritual life. This disposition, of course, was emulated perfectly by Mary, and therefore her life becomes a guide to our own relationship with God. Through Mary's life, I attempt to show, we can glimpse what it means to *"love the Lord your God with all your heart, and with all your soul, and with all your strength, and with all your mind; and your neighbor as yourself" (Luke 10:27)*.

One day I was sharing this retreat with a nun for whom I serve as spiritual director. After I was finished speaking, we paused for a moment, and then she casually said to me, "Why don't you turn it into a book?" A few seconds after she said this, I felt like I heard Mary say to me, "Yes, why don't you?" The following pages are my attempt to respond to what I perceived to be an inspiration coming from God, through his Holy Mother.

"Mary is not only an example for the whole Church in the exercise of divine worship but is also, clearly, a teacher of the spiritual life for individual Christians. The faithful at a very early date began to look to Mary and to imitate her in making their lives an act of worship of God and making their worship a commitment of their lives. As early as the fourth century, St. Ambrose, speaking to the people, expressed the hope that each of them would have the spirit of Mary in order to glorify God: 'May the heart of Mary be in each Christian to proclaim the greatness of the Lord; may her spirit be in everyone to exult in God.' But Mary is above all the example of that worship that consists in making one's life an offering to God."

—St. Pope Paul VI,
Marialis Cultus, February 2, 1974

"The more I imitate the Mother of God,
the more deeply I get to know God."

—St. Faustina

1

The Annunciation

Saying Yes to God

"*Behold, I am the handmaid of the Lord;*
let it be to me according to your word."
—*Luke 1:38*

TENSION BETWEEN CONTROL AND SURRENDER

Our relationship with God, like any relationship, is never static. It would be foolish and naïve to think that a relationship with God is a continual experience of nice feelings, pleasant experiences, and overwhelming clarity. It would also be foolish and naïve to think that a relationship with God consists of endless frustrations, recurring desolation, and countless dark nights. The truth is, in our relationship with God there is a consistent tension between control and surrender, or to put it more simply, between saying yes to God or saying no.

I would like to use the following analogy to help us understand, more realistically, what relationship with God looks like for most of us, much of the time.

Imagine you are driving a car and Jesus is sitting in the passenger seat with you. You look over at him as you are driving and are filled with gratitude that Jesus is in the passenger seat next to you. You love his company, you desire for him not only to be there but also to remain there, and perhaps you have even removed other people from the passenger seat so that Jesus can be there. While driving, you listen attentively to his advice regarding when to slow down, where to turn, and what direction you should take to arrive safely and speedily at your desired destination. During this whole time, you are deeply aware of his presence, and it leaves you feeling consoled, strengthened, and at peace. Everything feels right, life is good, especially with Jesus in the passenger seat.

However, an important truth needs to be mentioned. You are still driving. Yes, you are aware of Jesus, you are listening to him, you are obedient to his commands, yet your hands are still on the wheel.

At a particular moment of your drive, and only God knows when, Jesus asks you to pull over. Since you love him and desire to be obedient to him, you pull over on the side of the road where he will ask you a very profound, frightening, and important question: *Will you let me drive?* At first, you hesitate because you cannot comprehend why that is even necessary. From your perspective everything seems fine; you are listening to Jesus and doing everything he says, therefore you cannot understand not only why he wants to drive, but how that will make any difference.

Nonetheless, because you love Jesus, you smile at him and say, "Of course, Jesus, you can drive; here are the keys." After you switch seats and put on your seatbelts, Jesus pulls out onto the road as you begin adjusting to your new seat. Almost immediately, you realize how differently Jesus drives from you. He doesn't seem to obey all the traffic laws, at times he goes off the road, and at times it seems like he is even falling asleep at the wheel. After only being able to handle this for a few minutes, due to the incredible amount of fear and doubt this has caused within you, you rescind your yes to him and ask him to pull over. Once again now at the side of the road, you ask Jesus to give you the keys so that you can drive, because after all, you feel safer and more in control when you are driving and Jesus is in the passenger seat.

In your response to drive again, Jesus looks at you with deep compassion in his eyes and simply says to you, "Okay, you can drive, and I will go back to being a passenger."

This little story or analogy is what relationship with God looks like for most of us, much of the time. It is a tension and struggle between surrender and control, between saying yes or saying no.

Our salvation began because somebody gave God the keys and never asked for them back. In other words, somebody said yes to God and never changed her mind. She never doubted, or despaired and never tried to control. That someone, of course, is Mary.

MARY'S YES

Since the beginning of time, humanity has often and continues often to say no to God. For many people, this no to God is not said directly and emphatically, nor is it often a conscious and willed response to God from the depths of one's heart. In many ways, this "no" is simply the result of a poor and fragile humanity that is desperately in need of a Savior.

Personally, I don't wake up each morning and desire or plan to say no to God. In fact, the first thing I do every morning is pray a "Morning Offering," where I essentially begin the day offering, "my prayers, works, joys, and sufferings of this day,"[2] to God. In short, the Morning Offering is an echo of my own personal desire to say yes to God, through all the circumstances and situations I may find myself in throughout this new day. Unfortunately, the mere desire to offer everything to God does not imply that I will actually do it. The truth of the matter is that often a few minutes later, and some days even seconds later, this "yes" I have just made to God is already being tempted to waver.

I must struggle, as we all must, with my own weakness, laziness, selfishness, etc., all of which influences my heart and mind in such mysterious ways that one thing is certain: there is very rarely an unconditional and unequivocal YES given to God from his creatures.

There is, of course, one exception to this rule, and again, it is Mary. Mary's entire life is an unconditional and unequivocal yes to God. Mary does not say "yes" to God only once in her life. Rather, through every moment of her life, as we will see throughout this book, Mary's yes to God is renewed, continued, and deepened. Even though Mary's yes to God is continuous, the first time we hear that "yes" in the Scriptures occurs at the Annunciation, when the angel Gabriel appears to Mary and invites her to be the instrument of the

Incarnation of the Son of God, and hence, the instrument of the salvation of the world.

One of my favorite titles of Mary, and one of the oldest, is "Mary, the New Eve." Why is Mary called "the New Eve"? In Genesis we hear both Adam and Eve say no to God by eating of the tree of the knowledge of good and evil (Genesis 3:3). In contrast to their disregard for God's command, which basically is them saying, "I will drive, I will determine where I am going, and how I will get there," Mary at the Annunciation responds in an entirely different manner: *"Behold, I am the handmaid of the Lord; let it be to me according to your word."* Whereas Adam and Eve said no to God, Mary says yes, and her yes reverses the no of Adam and Eve. Hence, Mary is the New Eve!

As I mentioned earlier, the title of "Mary as the New Eve" is one of the oldest titles we have for her. In the second century St. Irenaeus wrote: *"The knot of Eve's disobedience was untied by Mary's obedience: what the Virgin Eve bound through her disbelief, Mary loosened by her faith."* In the fourth century St. Jerome succinctly summarizes this truth by declaring: "Death through Eve, life through Mary."

Through Mary's yes God continues the work of salvation. What else is the work of salvation other than God continuing to reveal his love for us? This time, through Mary's yes, this profound love of God will be revealed in the most astonishing way: through the Incarnation of the Son of God. There are many reasons why we should love Mary, but if somebody said to me, "Give me one reason why you love Mary and why you should," I would simply answer by saying: because she gives us Jesus!

Through her yes, the one who will *"reconcile to himself all things"* (*Colossians 1:20*) begins to take flesh in Mary. The great mystery, the great "secret" of God in Christ begins because somebody trusts God enough and because somebody believes and loves him unlike any other.

What then does Mary's yes consist of? It is, essentially, a yes to the Holy Trinity. It is a yes to the will of the Father. It is a yes to receiving the Son. And it is a yes to the action of the Holy Spirit. This is simply a theological way of saying that Mary's yes is perfect.

In the votive Mass entitled *"Holy Mary, the New Eve,"* the Prayer after Communion emphasizes this truth: In that prayer we say, *"Lord, our God, in the Blessed Virgin Mary you formed a new heart for the second Eve; grant that by the grace of this Sacrament we may be obedient to the inspiration of the Holy Spirit and grow more and more each day in the likeness of Christ, the second Adam."* What are we asking for in that prayer? That Mary's will become our own, and that we will be obedient to the will of the Father. This consists in receiving Jesus, in being molded more and more in his likeness. And for that to occur we must also say yes to the Holy Spirit, who is the only One who can bring this about.

This, and so much more, is what Mary's yes contains.

THE YES TO SALVATION IN OUR LIFE

After considering all this, let us reflect about the work of salvation in our own personal lives. St. Paul tells us, *"For the Son of God, Jesus Christ, whom we preached among you, Silvanus and Timothy and I, was not Yes and No, but in Him it is always yes. For all the promises of God find their Yes in him"* (2 Corinthians 1:19–20).

Jesus's entire life is a yes; Mary's life, as we have begun to see and will continue to see throughout her entire life, is a yes. What are we right now in our life? What are our actions, thoughts, prayers, and desires saying? Are we Yes or are we No? Most likely, many of us are more like "I don't know." Even though we don't want to say no to God, our own weakness and fear often prevent us from saying yes, and so we often end up in the middle.

Why do we hesitate so much in saying yes to God? If the will of God is our ultimate good, why are we not more confident and courageous in saying yes to it? Perhaps one of the reasons we find both God and his will mysterious is that he doesn't ask for our opinion or our advice. Nor should he. God, through the angel Gabriel, does not say to Mary, "You know, Mary, I'm thinking about doing something great through you, and I just wanted to know what you thought about that." This is not the way God operates. God is not interested in opinion polls and whether we will like something or not. Rather, the angel Gabriel says to Mary, *You will conceive in your womb and bear a son and you shall call his name Jesus" (Luke 1:31).* In other words, the angel Gabriel is presenting God's will to Mary and asking her to say yes to it. He is not asking her to say yes to her will or her version of God's will, but to say yes to and participate in God's plan of salvation for her and for the whole world.

St. Bernard, writing of Mary, was deeply aware of the worldwide implications that God's will had for Mary when he wrote:

> *The price of our salvation is offered to you. We shall be set free at once if you consent. . . . In your brief response we are to be remade in order to be recalled to life. . . . Tearful Adam with his sorrowing family begs this of you, O loving Virgin. . . . Abraham begs it, David begs it, all the other holy patriarchs, your ancestors, ask it of you. . . . This is what the whole world waits for, prostrate at your feet. . . . On your word depends . . . salvation for all the sons of Adam, the whole of your race.*[3]

What is St. Bernard "reminding" Mary and us of? God's will is always bigger than us. God's will doesn't just include us, but literally has worldwide implications. Think for a moment about all the people God's will for you has affected. Whether you are married, a priest or religious, or whether you are living in the world, God's will in your life includes countless numbers of people, many of whom you are probably not even aware of.

When I walk into a store or walk through a town, I am always wearing my gray Franciscan habit. Even though I might not talk to anyone, many people stop and stare, simply because they are not used to seeing monks in public. Regardless of what people think I am, they are aware, at the very least, that I am a religious person, which, if only for a second, causes them to reflect on a reality beyond this world. If I were dressed in jeans and a T-shirt, this most likely would not happen, but since God's will for me is to be a Franciscan, and part of being a Franciscan means wearing a gray robe, simply walking in a store or through a town influences everyone there.

What then is the conclusion here? God's will is not just about you. So, of course God is not going to seek our advice and opinion when it comes to his will and our salvation. Inside God's will (his plan of salvation), there is so much beauty and love, and it is so profound that we can't even begin to fathom it. We literally have no clue of the profundity of God's will in our life. If you gathered the 100 most intelligent people in the world and had them construct a plan for your life and you told them your talents, dreams, desires, etc., that plan would be infinitely inferior to the beauty and depth that is God's will for your life. God's will in our life is the "perfect life"; it is a life of mesmerizing beauty and tremendous depth.

Often, we hear people speak or dream about the "perfect life." Hollywood and the world of advertising would like us to believe that their story or their product is exactly what is missing in our life. If we only dress a certain way, act a certain way, or live a certain way, then our lives too can become perfect. Hence, the phrase "a perfect life" is often presented as a superficial existence that consists of a life of ease, pleasure, and comfort. However, we often forget that, contrary to Hollywood and the advertising world, the perfect life has already been given to us in God's will.

What Our Lady teaches us is that our life is more beautiful and profound when we allow it to be navigated by God's will—in other words, when we are saying YES to God! When we say yes to God this is when and how real transformation occurs. A yes to God opens our hearts, our minds, and our whole being to the presence of God in a way that nothing else can. Because of Mary's continual yes to God in her life, she will possess a deeper and more intimate knowledge and experience of God than any theologian, any religious person, or any other person in human history. Nobody knows God like Mary!

Could she have been like this is if she had said no? The answer is no. Her yes opens her heart, her mind, and her whole being to the beauty and the mystery of God. The same is true for us.

Caryll Houselander once wrote: *"In surrendering to the Spirit . . . Mary wed God to the human race and made the whole world pregnant with the life of Christ."*[4] Certainly, Mary's yes is unique, but when we say yes to God and surrender to the Spirit, we too give birth to Christ in the world, to people in our ministry, our community, and the people we share life with.

It would not be too dramatic to say that the whole world needs your yes to God. I need it, your family members need it, the people you work with need it, your neighbors, and all the strangers that you pass on the street each day need your yes to God. Why? Because your yes makes Christ present and visible. Don't we all need to see Christ more deeply?

MARY'S ADVICE

Considering all this, what then would Mary's advice be to us? It is, I believe, both strengthening and encouraging. Imagine if we were speaking with her in the context of spiritual direction.

Imagine for a moment that Mary is your spiritual director. What would that be like for you? This is the way I imagine it for myself.

I am sitting with Mary in a room overlooking a lake. On the wall is a simple crucifix and we are seated on two simple wooden chairs. I begin by expressing to her all my fears, my desires, my hopes, my wounds, my weaknesses, etc. All the while she is listening very attentively and with deep compassion in her eyes.

When I am finished, we sit there together in silence and gaze out the window at the lake. After a few moments she looks me in the eye and says, "My son, God is trustworthy. Don't be afraid to say yes to him. Don't wait for consolation, don't wait for understanding, don't wait for everyone to agree with you, and don't wait until everything in your life is 'perfect,' because it never will be. Say yes to him today, and then tomorrow, and again every day, because he is trustworthy, and he is faithful."

2

The Visitation

Marian Spirituality

"Blessed are you among women and blessed is the fruit of your womb!"
—*Luke 1:42*

MARIAN SPIRITUALITY

E ven though I was born and raised Catholic, like many teenagers I drifted away from the Church for a few years. I never considered myself an atheist or even agnostic, and if someone were to ask me during this time if I believed in God, I would have responded emphatically by saying yes. The simple reason I stopped going to church was because, like many people, I got distracted. I found music, traveling, and writing, more fulfilling and even more "spiritual" than praying and attending Mass.

However, shortly after I graduated from high school, I experienced a "reversion" to the Catholic faith while driving across the country with a few friends. During this time, the beauty of the natural world and my own restlessness for something more led me to begin to pray for the first time in years. Shortly after I uttered that first prayer, I found myself in line one Saturday afternoon for confession at a random Catholic parish in Kansas, and later that day, walking forward to receive the Eucharist during Mass. My life was instantly changed.

When I returned from that trip, I immediately began devouring books on prayer and spirituality so that I could grow in this newfound relationship with God I had just discovered. I applied things I learned from Carmelite spirituality, Benedictine spirituality, and Franciscan spirituality. However, I felt that something was missing. Not sure what exactly it was, I asked myself one day, "How did I come to know Jesus?" Almost immediately I answered, *Mary.* It was Mary I turned to and prayed to in those first moments of my reversion, and it was Mary, I believe, who led me to confession and back to Mass.

Despite how clear and obvious this was to me, I thought that maybe I was being too subjective and therefore needed a more objective criterion to determine exactly what was missing in my spirituality. This time I asked myself, "How did Jesus come to us?" Once again, I immediately answered by saying, *Mary*. It was then that I realized first and foremost that my spirituality had to be Marian, not because I considered it beautiful and that it was fruitful, though it was certainly both, but because Mary was the way Jesus chose to reveal himself to us.

St. Paul confirms this when he says, *"When the time had fully come, God sent forth his Son, born of a woman"* (Galatians 4:4). Hence, there is no other way in which Jesus came to us except through Mary. Considering this biblical and theological truth, St. Louis de Montfort says, *"Therefore, if we wish to go to him, seeking union with him, we must use the same means which he used in coming down from heaven to assume our human nature. . . . That means was a complete dependence on Mary his Mother."*[5]

St. Louis de Montfort is reminding us of something very important regarding the Incarnation: namely, there is nothing random about it. The way and the circumstances in which God would become man were not accidental or coincidental. Since Mary was the way in which God would become man, we can also therefore conclude that Mary was not accidental or coincidental. She was deliberately chosen. In other words, Mary, in the plan of God, was chosen to bring us Jesus, and not just at one moment in time, but until eternity.

When I was in college, I was friendly with a wonderful group of very sincere Christians who, though not Catholic, were very respectful toward me and considered me a real disciple of Jesus, even though many of them were confused about Catholic teaching. One Friday night, after a Bible study with this group, my friend Dan and I were walking back to the dorms, and he started asking me questions about Mary, specifically why Catholics believe that Mary is so important. After almost an hour of discussion using the Bible and theology to prove our points, he finally said to me, "I don't need Mary, I have Jesus." To which I replied, "Ok, maybe you don't, but

Jesus did, and aren't we supposed to imitate him?" After this little exchange, we never talked about Mary again, because I believe, he saw the logic and the theological consistency of why Mary is important.

Considering then the historical and theological reality of the Incarnation, St. Louis de Montfort concludes by saying, *"She (Mary) is the safest, easiest, shortest and most perfect way of approaching Jesus."*[6]

MARY, THE ARK OF THE NEW COVENANT

Everything we have been reflecting on thus far is affirmed so beautifully in the Gospel account of the Visitation. In this biblical account, Mary, in her very womb, is bringing Jesus to Elizabeth and Zechariah. Mary's visit to her cousin Elizabeth is not merely an opportunity to provide Elizabeth, who is also pregnant, with moral support and encouragement, though that is present also. Mary's visit to Elizabeth is a visitation from God.

To understand more deeply who Mary is and to understand the significance of the Visitation we must turn to the Old Testament. If we read the Gospel account of the Visitation alongside 2 Samuel 6, we find a striking similarity that leads us to a profound and beautiful conclusion. In 2 Samuel 6, King David is bringing the Ark of the Covenant to Jerusalem. The Ark of the Covenant, as you may remember, contained the two stone tablets on which the Ten Commandments were written and therefore was the sign of God's presence among his people. Hence, King David is entrusted with an important mission, to bring the ark of the covenant, that is, the presence of God, to the people.

In 2 Samuel 6:2 we read, *"David arose and went with all the people who were with him from Baale-judah, to bring up from there the ark of God."* In Luke 1:39, we read, *"Mary arose and went with haste into the hill country, to a city of Judah."* In 2 Samuel 6:9 David asks, *"How can the ark of the* Lord *come to me?"* In Luke 1:43 after greeting Mary, Elizabeth asks, *"Why is this granted me, that the mother of my Lord should come to me?* In 2 Samuel 6:15–16 we are told that *"David . . . brought up the ark of the* Lord *with shouting, and with the sound of the horn . . ."* and was *"leaping and dancing before the* Lord*."* In Luke 1:41–42 we are told that at the sound of Mary's voice, John the Baptist *"leaped in her (Elizabeth's) womb; and Elizabeth was filled with the Holy Spirit and she exclaimed with a loud cry, 'Blessed are you among women, and blessed is the fruit of your womb.'"* Finally, in 2 Samuel 6:11 we are told that *"the ark of the* Lord *remained in the house of Obed-edom the Gittite three months,"* and in Luke 1:56 we are told that Mary *"remained with her (Elizabeth) about three months."*

What is all this implying? Could it be a mere biblical coincidence? Of course not. St. Luke is trying to tell us and show us that Mary is the new dwelling place of God, that she is the Ark of the New Covenant. The Ark of the Old Covenant, as I mentioned, was the visible sign for the people of the Old Testament of the invisible God, the very presence of God in their midst. Now, Mary is the Ark of the New Covenant because she carries in herself the presence of the invisible God who is about to made visible through her.

Therefore, St. Athanasius says that Mary is *"God's place of repose."* She is the place where God found no resistance, doubt, or selfishness, but instead found faith, hope, and love, in abundance and in total and complete purity. St. Paul says to the Colossians, *"Let the word of Christ dwell in you richly" (Colossians 3:16)*. Mary fulfilled those words long before St. Paul ever wrote them and will continue to fulfill them for all eternity.

Also, in the Old Testament, God led the Israelites to the Promised Land through a pillar of cloud by day and at night by a pillar of fire.

The LORD went before them by day in a pillar of cloud to lead them along the way, and by night in a pillar of fire to give them light, that they might travel by day and by night; the pillar of cloud by day and the pillar of fire by night did not depart from before the people.
—*Exodus 13:21–22*

With the advent of the New Covenant, God would no longer guide his people in the former manner. Now the presence of God is being revealed through the lowly and humble presence of Mary. This, of course, is not merely a one-time historical event, but is what Mary will continue to do throughout all human history, including of course in our own personal lives, to the extent that we allow her. In the last few centuries Mary has been appearing in places like Mexico City, Lourdes, Fatima, and many other places to various cultures and ethnicities. Even though she often appears to poor children, her message is for all of humanity. What is her message in all these different apparitions? It is the same message she brought to her cousin Elizabeth: it is the message of the Gospel, which is not a theory or an ideal, but a person, Jesus!

As a priest, I often hear stories of people who have abandoned the faith or have left the Church for various reasons. Often these stories are told to me by a concerned parent, family member or friend. They come to me and share these heartbreaking stories because they are looking for and hoping for some sort of consolation. What they are basically asking from me is some sort of hope that their family member or friend will one day return to God and choose to live a holy life, rather than a secular life consumed primarily with self-interest.

I can sympathize deeply with them, since I, like everyone, have friends and family members who have stopped going to church. After all, I too, was one of those who stopped going to church for a time. My advice to them, which is also a reminder to myself, is always the same: pray to Mary every day for them and do not stop! In the *"Memorare"* prayer we recite these beautiful words to Mary, "Never was it known that anyone who fled to thy protection, implored thy help, was left unaided." Never was it known! Very powerful and bold words, and from my experience, and the experience of so many others, they are true.

Though God and Mary respect our free will, I am convinced one can only resist the purity, beauty, and holiness of Mary for so long. Her presence in our life, even if it is only through a short prayer or a quick glance at her in a statue or painting, is like the first streaks of dawn appearing on the horizon, announcing the beginning of a new day. The gentleness and beauty of the dawn helps to soften our heart and ease our anxiety about what this new day may bring. Within a month of my "reversion" I was praying the Rosary every day, attending daily Mass, and studying the Bible. Even though I had been away from Mass for years, had no idea how to pray, and felt overwhelmed merely holding a Bible, as I turned to her the fear and anxiety disappeared almost instantly. When people asked what happened to me, I looked at them a bit confused, yet filled with joy and said, "I don't know what happened—the woman is doing all of this!" The woman, of course, was Mary.

THE FRUITS OF MARIAN SPIRITUALITY

Having established thus far the significance of Mary and the need for a Marian spirituality, we can now ask ourselves, "How does Mary's presence in our lives affect us? What is the fruit of a Marian spirituality?" There are many ways in which Mary's presence in our lives affects us, just as there are many fruits possible to us because of Mary's presence in our lives, too many to be mentioned in any book. However, I would like to mention two that I believe are the most prominent.

***

The first fruit of Marian spirituality is peace. Mary calms our soul. When I was a child, my father, who is a wonderful man, was often working and tended toward anxiety. My mother was the exact opposite. Because she chose to stay home and raise my sister and me, she was always present and available. Even though my father would often worry about everything, my mother never worried about anything, and she always assured us that everything would be okay. Oddly enough, she was always right, and so my sister and I always turned to her when something was wrong. The effect this had on my sister and me was always the same. It brought us peace and calm.

Often peace has been described as "the absence of war," or as "the tranquility of order." Many people assume that they can experience peace if their life is organized and well mannered. Therefore, many people spend an enormous amount of time and energy trying to perfect the details of their life and avoid, at all costs, anything that could cause the slightest interruption or inconvenience. What is ironic is that by trying to perfect our lives with such intensity, we often create a life that is stressful and frustrating, the exact opposite of peace. Something more is needed if we hope to experience peace in our life.

True peace occurs only when we surrender ourselves to God's will. Jesus says, *"Whoever does the will of my Father in heaven is my brother, and sister, and mother" (Matthew 12:50).* When we embrace God's will and live it as best as we can, we experience peace. Peace has nothing to do with my social status, my age, or my health. If only it were that easy. Throughout my life I have known many rich, young, and healthy people who do not have peace, but are in fact quite miserable. There is nothing that Mary wants for us and helps us with more than the fulfillment of God's will in our lives. At the Wedding Feast of Cana, she tells the waiters, *"Do whatever he tells you" (John 2:5)*, and at the Annunciation she responds to God's will by saying, *"Let it be to me according to your word" (Luke 1:38)*. Mary's will and her only desire is God's will. She has no other agenda other than the will of God.

Fr. Emile Neubert in his book, *"Life of Union with Mary,"* writes:

> *Peace is the natural climate of Marian souls. . . . When Herod was seeking the newborn King to slaughter him, Jesus slept peacefully in the arms of His Mother on the way to Egypt. This is a perfect symbol of every Marian soul. Such a soul always reposes peacefully in the arms of its mother.*[7]

A fruit of Mary's presence in our life is peace, because Mary assists us in the only way that peace can occur: by embracing God's will in our life.

***

The second fruit of Marian spirituality is strength. The presence of Mary in our lives strengthens us. We witness this so clearly in the Gospel account of the Visitation. Elizabeth is strengthened by Mary's presence. *"When Elizabeth heard the greeting of Mary . . . [she] was filled with the Holy Spirit and she exclaimed with a loud cry, 'Blessed are you among women, and blessed is the fruit of your womb!'" (Luke 1:41–42)*.

For what does the presence of Mary strengthen Elizabeth, and us? Again, for God's will. Ultimately, it strengthens her and us for the fulfillment of God's will in her life, and this often results in the strength to offer a deeper yes to God, through his will. This strength that a Marian soul experiences is obviously, not for itself and its own ego, but it is ultimately oriented toward the completion and fulfillment of God's will in our life. In other words, Mary strengthens us to become who we are supposed to be in God. Mary is not here to strengthen us with our own ideas and agenda, but God's.

When I first experienced the call to the priesthood, like many young men who experience this call, I was afraid and thought I was crazy. *How could I be called to be a priest?* I thought. First, I am a sinner. Second, I am not a good public speaker, and finally, I don't have the practical gifts that I believe are necessary to help and guide the people of God in their life and in their relationship with God. I brought all these concerns to Mary each day, and much to my surprise, each day the fear and doubt that I first experienced when considering a vocation to the priesthood began to dissipate. A few months later, during my senior year in college, I decided after graduation I was going to enter the Franciscans and become a priest. After being a priest now for 11 years, I realize without any doubt that it was Mary who was and continues to strengthen me in this vocation that I am certainly not worthy of, but one which God, in his mercy, has given to me.

St. Maximilian Kolbe writes: *"The Immaculate is the highest degree of perfection and sanctity of a creature. . . . He who gives himself without limits to the Immaculate will in a short time attain a very high degree of perfection and procure for God a very great glory."*[8]

MARY IS FOR EVERYONE

Regardless then of what our spirituality is, whether it be Franciscan, Carmelite, Benedictine, etc., before all of that we are Marian. Of course, this will look different and be expressed in each person differently, but at our spiritual core, we are all Marian. A Marian spirituality is not merely one form of spirituality among others, but it is the one that has been given to us all by Jesus. A Franciscan, Carmelite or Benedictine spirituality is not given to all people, but a Marian spirituality is.

I was speaking with a friend recently and shared with him that I was currently writing a book on Mary. He appeared interested and asked me, "Who is the book for? Who is your intended audience?" I paused for a moment because, for some reason, I had never considered that question before. However, after reflecting for a moment I said to him with a smile on my face, "The book is for everyone, because Mary is for everyone."

3

The Magnificat

Our Need for God

"He has regarded the low estate
of his handmaiden."
—Luke 1:48

WE ARE IN NEED

As a priest, I have spoken with many different people over the years. Among these people, some were religious, some were atheist, and some were agnostic. I have spoken with rich and poor, young and old, sick and healthy, people of every race and ethnicity, people with doctor's degrees from prestigious universities, and people, like my father, who never finished high school. Throughout all these various conversations I have noticed a recurring theme in all of them: we are in need. Regardless of one's social status, belief system, or cultural background, I have never met one person in life who is complete in and of themselves. Of course, some people believe they are complete and in need of nothing, yet their lack of self-knowledge reveals they are just like everyone else: in need.

Over the years I have been blessed to accompany a few people who are in AA. I have nothing but respect and admiration both for the program itself and the people who are part of it. I once attended an AA meeting with a friend of mine who was too afraid to go by himself. After the meeting, my friend asked me what I thought, and I responded enthusiastically, "It was so refreshing." Throughout the meeting someone would stand up and basically say, "Hello, I'm Bob and my life is a mess." Then he would sit down, and a few moments later someone else would stand up and say, "Hello, I'm Kelly and my life is a mess." After hearing this for an hour, I remember thinking to myself that this is the most honest conversation I have heard in a very long time, and this led me to conclude that they have a higher level of self-knowledge and self-awareness than most people.

Unfortunately, most of us do not speak like this. Rather we say things like, "Hello, I'm Bob and I'm amazing. I make this much money; I have this many degrees, and I drive this kind of car. And by the way, my family is perfect, my church is perfect, and the school where my children go is perfect." We feel the need to impress others and to prove to others that we are in control of our lives. In short, we want people to believe that we are not in need of anything. Our greatest proof for this, we believe, is our external accomplishments. The reality is that those who spend their life talking and acting like this have little self-knowledge and self-awareness, and they could greatly benefit from attending a few AA meetings, regardless of whether they have a drug or alcohol addiction.

What compounds this problem even more is that there is nothing of this world that can complete us or that can satisfy this need. The more we try to use this world or the things of this world the more deeply we feel this need. Interestingly, this also includes our spiritual life, that is, our relationship with God. Prayer, spiritual reading, and the sacraments are all necessary for our spiritual life, yet even they do not take away this need. They console us, strengthen us, and orient our souls toward the One who can, yet they do not take away this need. In fact, a mature spiritual life acknowledges this need more honestly and humbly.

Today, if we say that somebody is "needy" we are usually referring to an imbalance in their psychological and emotional life. Hence, calling someone "needy" is never a compliment. However, being "needy" is a part of who we are, regardless of how organized our psychological and emotional life is and no matter how much we may have convinced others that we are different. The truth never changes: we are in need.

Typically, we do not respond to these truths very well. Often, when our neediness is presented before us, we almost automatically begin the blame game and point fingers. It's my parent's fault, my superior's fault, or my boss's fault, we say. To some extent, that may be true, but not completely. In other words, when our neediness is presented to us, we generally try to run from it or hide from it. Therefore, this is perhaps the most fundamental truth about us: we are in need of everything. How we respond to this truth will ultimately shape our lives and our destiny.

MARY KNOWS HER NEED

If there is anyone who knows her need for God and doesn't run from it or try to hide from it, it is Mary. In her Magnificat, Mary proclaims, *"My spirit rejoices in God my Savior, for he has regarded the low estate of his handmaiden" (Luke 1:47–48).* The word *handmaiden* is a word many of us are probably not familiar with. Generally, handmaiden refers to a personal maid or a female servant, generally implying a woman of lowly status. We never hear Mary complaining about her earthly lot or doubting God's love because of her lack of worldly prestige. Rather, Mary is describing herself as a servant of the Lord, one who is lowly and who needs a Savior. What is so strange about this, at least to most of us, is that this need causes her to rejoice. Never once does she deny it or try to fix it herself. Neither does she turn to the things of this world for a solution. On the contrary, her need leads her away from herself and out toward God, whom she knows and believes is the only One who can satisfy it.

Does your need cause you to rejoice in God your Savior? For most of us, the answer to that question is a resounding no! Often our need turns us inward and toward ourselves. We become insecure and defensive, and we start grasping at everything within reach—people, situations, and events—in the hopes that they will complete us and give us a feeling of fulfillment. In other words, instead of receiving life from God, we are now trying to control it and fulfill ourselves by our own means.

I spent most of my childhood and teenage years, unfortunately, living this way. Since my father was shot in his left shoulder in the Vietnam War, he only has use of one arm. Due to his injury, he was never able, unlike many other fathers I knew, to teach me how to fix and build things with my hands. I never learned how to change a tire, use a hammer, or drive stick shift. The older I got, the more deeply I felt my need. It was so bad that for a time when I was 17 years old, I experienced a great deal of fear and anxiety regarding life in general because of the overwhelming feeling that I was unprepared for what life could throw at me. All I knew and felt was my own neediness, and despite all my attempts to fix it myself, all my efforts ended in vain.

Why does Mary's need cause her to rejoice? Because she knows that Jesus is the whole reason for her existence. Mary never tries to be an independent person and have her own life. She doesn't follow trends and what is considered popular. She doesn't spend time building up her résumé and hoping to impress people by her accomplishments. She doesn't need to do any of this because Mary knows that Jesus, and only Jesus, completes the mystery that is Mary's life. Mary knows that she has no life apart from Jesus. In the Gospel of John, Jesus tells us, *"Apart from me, you can do nothing"* *(John 15:5)*. Mary not only knows this, but she also embraces it. She lives her whole life with and in God her Savior.

This can be further illustrated in all the Church's dogmatic teachings about Mary (her Divine Motherhood, Perpetual Virginity, Immaculate Conception, and Assumption). All these teachings are based on her need for Jesus. For example, her Immaculate Conception is based upon the merits of her Son's passion, and her Assumption into heaven is the first fruits of his resurrection. All these dogmatic truths about Mary find their source and origin in Jesus, for the graces given to her are impossible by herself. Thomas Merton writes that Mary's *"highest privilege is her poverty, and her greatest glory is that she is most hidden, and the source of all her power is that she is nothing in the presence . . . of God."*[9]

What Mary does do, as we hear in her Magnificat, is embrace both her need and her Savior, in a way so profound and so beautiful, that to this day, her prophecy, *"All generations will call me blessed"* *(Luke 1:48)*, remains true. Mary shows us, both in word and in action that this need is intended by God, not to make us insecure and make us feel bad about ourselves, but to open us to the presence of God and our salvation. Hence, this need is meant to be not an empty space within us, but a place where God desires to dwell and to fill with his presence and love.

THE MAGNIFICAT

With all of this in mind, we can now take a deeper look into the song of praise that we call the Magnificat. To do so, we must take a closer look at Mary's words so that we can see and understand the depth of her song. The Magnificat consists of only nine verses. In those nine verses Mary references herself six times and God 18 times. Three of the times she references herself we hear her praising God: *"My soul magnifies the Lord, and my spirit rejoices in God my Savior" (Luke 1:46–47)*. The other three times she references herself, we hear her proclaiming God's work in her. *"He has regarded the low estate of his handmaiden. For behold, henceforth all generations will call me blessed; for he who is mighty has done great things for me" (Luke 1:48–49)*.

How different is Mary's Magnificat from most of the music and videos found in popular culture and on social media, where so often the emphasis is laid upon the individual and becomes nothing else but self-obsession. Mary not only sings a very different song, but she also sings it in a very different way. When Mary references herself, the words she utters are turned into praise. Even when Mary is talking about herself, she is praising God.

I heard a story once about a monk who many believed was a very holy man, and some even suggested that he was a living saint. When a visiting monk went to see him and returned to his monastery, all the monks he lived with were curious to know if all the reports were true. "Is it true, Father?" his fellow monks eagerly asked him. "Is he as holy as people say he is?" "My brothers," the visiting monk addressed his fellow monks, "I'm afraid to report that though he seems to be a good man, I do not think he is holy just yet." Feeling distraught over this monk's evaluation, one of them asked him, "How do you know that, Father?" The monk simply replied, "He talked about himself too much!"

Such a conclusion could never be made regarding Mary. In the twenty-seven books in the New Testament, only two, the Gospel of Luke and the Gospel of John, render words spoken by Mary. That means that Mary speaks in just less than eight percent of the New Testament, and in total she utters 183 words. Her only recorded words occur during the Annunciation, the Magnificat, the Finding of the Child Jesus in the Temple, and at the Wedding in Cana. It would be impossible to ever claim about Mary that she talked about herself too much.

Mary never wants to be thought of apart from God. Some people, both Catholic and Protestant, might be suspicious that too much attention to Mary will detract from Jesus or take away from the glory that is due to him. The Magnificat reveals to us that this is impossible. Also, it is important to mention that Mary does not have some secret ulterior motive. It is almost impossible for us to conceive of another person without at least a small amount of self-interest; however, in Mary we encounter such a person. She lives, breathes, speaks, and acts only for the glory of God. In other words, Mary lives entirely and purely for God alone.

Bishop Fulton Sheen captures this perfectly when he writes, *"Mary receives praise as a mirror receives light: she stores it not, nor even acknowledges it, but makes it pass from her to God to Whom is due all praise, all honor and thanksgiving. . . . Her whole personality is to be at the service of God."*[10] Hence, we never have to worry about Mary distracting us from Jesus.

Returning to the Magnificat, Mary references God 18 times. *"He who is mighty . . . holy is his name . . . his mercy is on those who fear him . . . he has shown strength with his arm . . . he has put down the mighty from their thrones . . . he has filled the hungry with good things, etc."*

What do Mary's words tell us about her and God? They reveal to us that Mary understands who God is! Namely, that he alone is Savior, that he alone is her strength, that he alone completes her need, and that he does all these things—saves us, strengthens us, and completes our need—not from a distance, but in the presence of her Son, in whom *"we live and move and have our being"* (Acts 17:28). Throughout human history, many people have spoken about God as a distant Being who is not interested in the affairs of his creatures. Mary, in her Magnificat, sings a song about a very different God, a God who is close and whose primary interest is us, his beloved sons and daughters. In such a song, Mary is reminding us, then, not only to turn to God, but also to expect everything from him, and in the meantime to praise him, because he is faithful, and he is good.

MARY TEACHES US HOW TO LIVE WITH OUR NEED

What is Mary doing in all that we have considered thus far? She is living and embodying the Gospel. Jesus tells us, *"I am the way, and the truth, and the life; no one comes to the Father, but by me"* (John 14:6). Before Jesus even uttered those words, Mary believed and was already living this truth. St. Paul tells us, *"The Spirit helps us in our weakness; for we do not know how to pray as we ought* (Romans 8:26). Mary, by herself, did not know how to pray. However, she availed herself each day of the grace of God and experienced an interior depth with God that no person will ever know in this life.

The core message that Jesus and St. Paul are proclaiming, and in which Mary is living, can be summed up in what is essentially the essence of Baptism: adopted sonship. Through our baptism we have become children of God. *"See what love the Father has given us,"* St. John tell us, *"that we should be called children of God; and so we are"* *(1 John 3:1)*. As children of God, we, like all children, are **always** dependent, not the way a slave is dependent on his master, but the way a child is dependent on his parents for everything. Unlike children in this world, in our relationship with God we never grow up; we are always sons and daughters. *"Unless you turn and become like children, you will never enter the kingdom of heaven"* *(Matthew 18:3)*.

As beautiful as this may sound, most of us struggle with it. We want to perfect ourselves by ourselves. We want to appear to everyone, whether in our religious communities, our families, or the towns we live in, that we have it together. There is perhaps nothing more humiliating for us, and nothing that makes us so insecure, as the experience of incompetence or weakness. When we experience this within ourselves and others in life, we must be extremely gentle and patient. However, we must also realize and accept the fact that neither we nor anyone else have our lives perfectly together, despite what might be portrayed externally. You and I do not have our lives together, and the good news is, we don't need to. That is why we have a Savior, and that Savior is not you or I, or any other person. It is only Jesus. No matter how successful we may be in this world, we will always need a Savior, since by ourselves, we are incomplete.

Because I am a priest, preaching is an essential and daily activity that I am involved in. Even after being a priest and preaching for over ten years, I still do not feel like I know what I am doing, and I still struggle with knowing how to proclaim God's word to people, especially in a way that they can understand and that will be helpful for them in their lives. Every time I am about to preach, I take responsibility. I pray, reflect, and study. Yet, I always remind Jesus, "These are your people. If you want them to learn anything you are going to have to speak through me, because by myself, I have nothing."

So often we want to give God our best, as we should. So often we want to do great things for God, as we should. Yet, if we do not surrender to this fundamental need for him in everything, we ultimately have nothing to give God and we will never be able to do anything for God. After all, God is not a ruthless taskmaster who will only repay us based upon our productivity. Whether we perform well or not, whether we have much to give God or nothing, the call from Jesus always remains the same: *"Come to me, all who labor and are heavy laden, and I will give you rest" (Matthew 11:28).*

Thankfully, we do not need to pretend in our relationship with Jesus. We do not need makeup to cover over our imperfections or search frantically for a solution. Discipleship is not a performance. Rather, it is surrendering our need for him and to him each day and each moment. This is where our strength comes from, and this is where true joy can be found. Although this might appear difficult to believe and to accept, Mary reveals to us that it is true. May we become more like her and surrender our need to God more deeply each day.

4

The Birth of Jesus

Abandonment to Divine Providence

"She gave birth to her first-born son and wrapped him in swaddling cloths, and laid him in a manger, because there was no place for them in the inn."
—Luke 2:7

HISTORY: REDEEMED OR ABSURD?

My life, like so many others, was greatly affected by the events of 9/11. I was a senior in college on that terrible day and watched the news from my dorm room as the terror of that morning unfolded. Hours after the attack, I remember walking around campus feeling utterly stunned by those events, but also afraid about the future. I asked myself so many questions: "Is this the beginning of a new war?" "If somebody can fly a plane into a building, are any of us safe anymore?" "What does this mean for my own future and the future of this country?" Unfortunately, these questions have now become commonplace.

History affects how we live, not just today, but also in the future. For some, world events and their own personal history will lead them down a dark and narrow road filled with despair, addictions, atheism, and an overwhelming sense of hopelessness, both for the world and themselves. For others, it will lead them down a road that is both bright and open, where they will choose hope, trust, faith, and a life of confidence and strength, not just to humanity, but ultimately to God.

The French philosopher Jean-Paul Sartre (1905–1980) lived according to the belief that life is absurd. He held that everything in life is random; there is no God guiding history or watching over humanity. Therefore, there is no meaning behind the events of history and no real hope that life will ever be different. There is, simply put, nothing. One of his most famous quotes is that "hell is other people," a position that clearly reveals the dark and narrow path by which he chose to live.

Around the same time a Polish Franciscan priest named Maximilian Kolbe (1894–1941) was sent by the Nazis to Auschwitz, where he would eventually offer his life for another prisoner. This prisoner for whom he died was a married man with children, and St. Maximilian's heroic act of love gave this man at least the hope that he would live and one day be reunited with his family. How could St. Maximilian choose such a heroic and selfless act? What was different about him from Jean-Paul Sartre? St. Maximilian Kolbe, unlike Sartre, did not believe that life was absurd, or that hell was other people. Rather, he believed that there was a God guiding history and watching over humanity, despite the absolute horror he witnessed. He believed that it was his vocation, as a Christian, a priest, and a Franciscan to stand before the Nazis, and really the whole world, and proclaim the truth that Jesus Christ is the Lord of history.

What St. Maximilian Kolbe did was simply imitate Mary. Mary, as we have seen so far, in her Annunciation, in the Visitation, in her Magnificat, and now at the birth of Jesus, is proclaiming that Jesus Christ is the Lord of history. By proclaiming this truth, she is reminding us that despite how mysterious, painful, and confusing history can be, God is present in it and through it. How she proclaims this good news is deeply important for our own lives.

THE CIRCUMSTANCES AND SITUATION OF THE BIRTH OF JESUS

St. Luke tells us in his account of the birth of Jesus that, *"Joseph . . . went up from Galilee . . . to the city of David, which is called Bethlehem . . . to be enrolled with Mary . . . who was with child (Luke 2:4–5).* St. Luke wants to be very clear that Mary is traveling with Joseph. Why is that important? Because St. Luke is attempting to show us that God is using the events of human history to further our salvation. In other words, God is in the very mix of human history and not beyond it or aloof from it. For God, human history is a part of his saving plan.

The historical reason for Mary traveling to Bethlehem is the census made by Caesar Augustus. Since she is married to Joseph, Mary is obliged to be present with her husband to enroll in the census, despite her condition. Her journey to Bethlehem serves a providential or divine purpose. With Mary in Bethlehem (pregnant with Jesus), an ancient prophecy concerning Bethlehem as the birthplace of the Messiah can now be fulfilled: *"But you, O Bethlehem Eph'rathah, who are little to be among the clans of Judah, from you shall come forth for me one who is to be ruler in Israel, whose origin is from of old, from ancient days" (Micah 5:2).*

God is using history for our salvation. Through these events that occur in Bethlehem we are reminded how intimately God is involved in every detail and moment in our life. There is nothing that escapes his notice, nor is there anything beyond his grasp. The psalmist captures this truth most beautifully when he says, *"Where shall I go from your Spirit? Or where shall I flee from your presence? If I ascend to heaven, you are there! If I make my bed in Sheol, you are there!" (Psalm 139:7–8).* Furthermore, what this also reveals to us is that life is not absurd. If we can see with the eyes of faith we will encounter a deeply consoling truth: Not only is God guiding human history, and our own personal history, but also his presence is leading us through both.

When we consider 9/11, or any other events in history, it would be worthwhile to examine where God was during those moments. Such a question, when prayerfully considered, can have enormous effects in our life, not only for the present moment, but also for the future. When we prayerfully consider those moments, we are confronted with the horror and fear that they caused, but we are also, in a mysterious way, led to an awareness of the presence of God, even amidst such difficulties. An awareness of the presence of God not only can give us peace here and now but it also can give us confidence and hope regarding the future and all that may occur in history and in our own experience. If God is present here, we might ask, even amidst these difficult moments, then why would he not continue to be present in the future, regardless of what it may entail?

Though many of the details about Mary's journey to Bethlehem are unknown to us, one thing is certain: there was nothing comfortable or convenient about what was being asked of her. Traveling, especially while pregnant and even more so in those days, was never a comfortable experience. She lived purely and entirely through the eyes of faith, and therefore she believed and saw God amidst all the events of daily life, even when those events were difficult and caused her suffering, confusion, and heartache.

There is an extremely important spiritual truth here that Mary is trying to teach us. That truth is simply this: God uses everything to get to us. Everything! Nothing is random. Every moment of life contains an astonishing supernatural depth to it. This depth is so profound that our mind and senses are for the most part unable to comprehend the significance of each moment of our lives. That is why St. Paul counsels us to *"walk by faith, not by sight" (2 Corinthians 5:7).* Walking by faith, as Mary shows us, is the surest path to union with God, since it enables us to go far beyond the limitations of our own mind and what our senses can perceive.

ABANDONMENT TO DIVINE PROVIDENCE

If all we have been reflecting on thus far is true, then it appears there is only one way to live: abandonment to divine providence. In other words, abandonment to the way life really is, with all the circumstances and situations of our life, with all the people in our life, and with all the joys and sorrows that the present moment may contain. Why? Because that is where God is. By abandoning ourselves to divine providence we are proclaiming, not necessarily that I like everything that is happening in my life right now, but that I am choosing to believe that wherever I am, God is.

Jean-Pierre de Caussade in his wonderful book, *Abandonment to Divine Providence*, says this about Mary:

> *No matter what her jobs were—ordinary, commonplace, or seemingly more important ones—they revealed to her, sometimes quite clearly, sometimes obscurely, the activity of God and were an opportunity for her to praise God. Filled with joy, she regarded everything she had to do or suffer at any moment of her life as a gift from him who showers delights upon those who hunger and thirst only for him and not for the things of this world.*"[11]

What Fr. de Caussade is saying about Mary is that she continually lived in the presence of God and was therefore able to see through the things of this world. By continually living in the presence of God, she was able to see through her own life, with all its events and circumstances. What was she able to see? Namely, God! In other words, by seeing through the visible, she was led to the invisible; by seeing through created things, she was led to the Creator. This is how each one of us is called to live. St. Paul confirms this when he writes: *"We look not to the things are seen but to the things that are unseen, for the things that are seen are transient, but the things that are unseen are eternal"* (2 Corinthians 4:18).

If we are truly called to live our lives seeing through the visible to the invisible, how then can we live like this, practically speaking, especially since the invisible is not a concrete sense experience most of the time? What could this way of life demand from us? The answer is both simple, yet difficult. It demands that we trust. Abandonment to divine providence implies that we trust that through everything that happens to us in life, that God, somehow and in some way, is mysteriously at work, beneath it all, through it all, and in it all.

This is how Mary lived every moment of her life, in total and complete abandonment to divine providence. We witness this in her response to the angel Gabriel during the Annunciation and see it here at the fulfillment of that promise with Jesus' birth. After receiving those piercing words of Simeon at the Presentation, and after finally finding her Son after losing him for three days, Mary, once again, abandons herself to divine providence in each moment, trusting that God is present and mysteriously at work. Perhaps the most profound place this occurs is at the Cross, where she must witness her Son and her God spit on, mocked, and crucified. Even here, while her heart is broken and she is filled with grief, she once again abandons herself to divine providence. *The Catechism of the Catholic Church* expresses this truth beautifully when it states, *"Throughout her life and until her last ordeal when Jesus her Son died on the cross, Mary's faith never wavered. She never ceased to believe in the fulfillment of God's word. And so the Church venerates in Mary the purest realization of faith" (CCC 149)*. In other words, Mary is continually seeing through the visible, trusting ultimately in God's providence, and is therefore always living in his presence.

As Jesus is born in Bethlehem the first thing he will see when he opens his eyes in this world is a soul completely abandoned to divine providence. In the pure and loving gaze of Mary his mother he witnesses one who, like him, is surrendered to the will of the Father, through the utter mystery of God's providence. What a consolation that must have been for Jesus. Throughout his earthly life and teaching, Jesus would not experience such abandonment from anyone else to such a degree that he found in his mother. Throughout history, and still today, what Jesus experiences from most people are their doubts and suspicions, their self-centered and narrow judgments and criticisms, their own agendas and ideas, and their own will. None of this is present in Mary. She sees through it all. St. Lawrence Justinian says, *"Mary was not led by her own senses, nor by her own will; thus she accomplished outwardly through her body what wisdom from within gave to her faith.*"[12]

THE EYES OF MARY

If this then was the way in which Mary lived her relationship with God, imagine what our relationship with God would look like if we imitated her. Imagine for a moment how consoling it would be to God if we continued to pray, even when our prayer is dry and even when God appears absent. Imagine for a moment how consoling it would be to God if we chose to trust him, when everything around us, all the events and circumstances of life, were naturally causing suspicion and doubt within us. Imagine for a moment how consoling it would be to God if we saw through our own brokenness and poverty, and chose to believe in the love of God for us. If we lived like this, our lives would be very different. Therefore, what we need most in our relationship with God is the eyes of Mary.

Recently I was speaking with a very good friend of mine who raised four boys. During the discussion, we began speaking about Mary, and suddenly, my friend uttered these simple and profound words, "I couldn't have raised my boys without the eyes of Mary." I immediately froze upon hearing these words. She continued speaking, but I couldn't hear anything she was saying. The words "the eyes of Mary" penetrated deeply into my heart, and I thought to myself, *That is it, that is what I need, that is what we all need, the eyes of Mary!*

I asked her to repeat that line until I finally began to understand what she meant. Naturally, there is a great amount of fear and insecurity that occurs from simply raising one child, let alone four boys. What would she do when they got sick? How would she manage if God forbid, something happened to her or her husband? What will become of them in life? These and so many more questions would occupy her motherly heart each day. Yet what enabled my friend to navigate through such questions was viewing her life through Mary's eyes. It was Mary, she said, who helped her to see God in all the fear and insecurity that is present in life, especially in her vocation as a mother. And it was Mary, she said, who always provided an answer to the many questions that surface in a mother's heart. What was the answer that Mary always provided? It was the simple truth that God is always present in every circumstance and in every situation. This answer might not have solved every problem she would experience as a mother directly; however, it was an answer that strengthened her and enabled her to keep moving forward.

Ultimately, when my friend said, "I couldn't have raised my boys without the eyes of Mary," she was not merely speaking a truth that she found helpful. She was speaking a truth that is applicable and necessary for everyone, regardless of their vocation, whether one is celibate, married, or single: This truth is that through the eyes of Mary, we see Jesus as he really is, and where he really is. Who is Jesus in the eyes of Mary? He is the Living God in our midst. Where is Jesus in the eyes of Mary? Wherever you and I are.

5

Shepherds and Angels

The Marian Posture

"Mary kept all these things, pondering them in her heart."
—Luke 2:19

LISTENING

After spending nine years studying for the priesthood, I was ordained a priest on May 14, 2011. In January of 2012, I returned to school. However, this time I would be studying spiritual direction, a subject I was deeply interested in and felt God was calling me to. Each day in this spiritual direction program was relatively the same. In the morning we discussed the theory of spiritual direction, its history, and the many different forms it has taken throughout Church history. We studied the various schools of spirituality within Christianity and the impact they have had on the Church at large. We spent hours reflecting on spiritual truths such as consolation, desolation, the dark night of the soul, and so many other spiritual realities that saints and mystics articulated to help us navigate through the many struggles and trials we face toward a greater union with God.

The afternoons, however, looked very different. After lunch we assembled back into the classroom, put away our books, and began doing spiritual direction. This took place, to our dismay, in front of the whole class. Each one of us was paired up with another student, and one was assigned to be the director, while the other was the directee. Once we were finished, we switched roles so nobody was left out. The directee was instructed to discuss with their director what their experience of prayer was like in the past 24 hours. Even though we were in school, each student was required to pray three hours a day with various Scripture passages, all of which had a specific theme and grace attached to it. Hence, there was always an ample amount of content to share with one's spiritual director, whoever it might be that day.

The person who was the spiritual director was instructed thus: "You are not allowed to speak until your directee is finished, and then all you are allowed to do is summarize what your directee just shared. If your directee approves of your summary, then, and only then, can you continue. Then spiritual direction can begin." The first day I heard this rule I was utterly confused. *What do you mean, I'm not allowed to talk, I thought to myself. If I'm going to be a spiritual director, it's because I have something to say and teach others.* Or so I thought.

Thankfully, after days and weeks of repeating this exercise each afternoon, I began to understand what my teachers were trying to instill in us as future spiritual directors. They were trying to teach us, first and foremost, to be good listeners, because without listening, as I began to realize, there is no spiritual direction. As intimidating, and I must admit, annoying as this experience was at first, it became for me a profound and humbling experience of deep listening to another person, which became, ultimately, a deep experience of listening to God. This experience, and the entire spiritual direction program, was life-changing. It gave me what I refer to as a "contemplative orientation." The primary disposition in a contemplative orientation is listening. Everything else—activity, interpretations, and judgments—flows from this foundation.

This was not natural for me, and I tend to believe it is not natural for most of us. Often we approach life, whether it is prayer, ministry, or community life, with our ideas, interpretations, plans, opinions, desires, etc. We have something to offer, and we also want to receive something in return. Therefore, for most of us, our basic posture before life, and therefore, before God, is one of activity, namely, doing, thinking, and planning. Of course, doing, thinking, and planning are all necessities in life, but first we must listen.

Mary, as we will see, is the one, the only one, who truly listens to God. Her entire life flows from this contemplative orientation because she is rooted in a deep and profound listening to God.

MARY'S CONTEMPLATIVE POSTURE

In the Gospel passage we are reflecting on, St. Luke reports that a few poor shepherds are watching over their flock when suddenly an angel appears to them announcing the birth of Christ: *"Be not afraid.... I bring you good news of a great joy... to you is born ... a Savior.... This will be a sign for you: you will find a baby wrapped in swaddling cloths and lying in a manger"* (Luke 2:10–12).

Intrigued by the appearance of this angel and the news he has come to announce, the shepherds go to Bethlehem, finding everything exactly as the angel described. Immediately upon their arrival they tell Mary and Joseph all they have experienced. Even though many of us are familiar with this story, it is important to step back for a moment and reflect on the strange and mysterious nature of these events. Imagine for a moment if a stranger showed up at your house and said that an angel told them everything about the most intimate details about your life. How would you respond? I would respond not only with suspicion, but also with fear. Yet we are told that *"Mary kept all these things, pondering them in her heart"* (Luke 2:19).

How is Mary able to ponder these events in her heart? She can ponder them because she is listening, deeply listening with her whole being to everything occurring. Because she is deeply listening, she encounters and is able see the presence of God in all that is happening. How does she experience the presence of God? Not necessarily emotionally, psychologically, or in a sensible way. Rather, Mary's attentive listening enables her to perceive God in the depths of her heart, where she can say, at least interiorly, to all that is occurring, "It is the Lord."

This does not imply of course that Mary possesses perfect understanding or clarity of mind and vision. In many ways, none of this is necessary, because Mary's listening is rooted in faith, hope, and love. Since this is Mary's foundation, her listening extends far beyond the natural world and human reasoning. In other words, because Mary believes in God (not just with her head), and because she hopes and loves God so purely and so deeply, she is able to hear him, in all the mysterious and strange circumstances and situations that she is experiencing, not only here at the birth of Jesus, but throughout her entire life.

It could be easy to dismiss the profound nature of Mary's response to these events in Bethlehem. Some could argue, "Of course Mary responds perfectly. She is without sin and doesn't suffer from the effects of original sin like we all do. Therefore, Mary's response to God will always be perfect." Though it is true that Mary is *full of grace" (Luke 1:28)*, and that she always responds perfectly to God, it is also important to remember that Mary is fully human. This fullness of grace given to her does not allow her to coast through life on automatic pilot. She is affected in her heart and mind, and in her body and soul, by all the mysterious events and actions of her Son. In other words, she is always a mother who will always be affected by the life of her child. She must choose to participate each moment in the fullness of grace that was given to her. Without her participation, that is, her yes, that grace given to her cannot take effect. The same is true, of course, for us.

To illustrate this more clearly, we must consider the circumstances in which Mary gives birth to Jesus. Mary is not hidden away at a retreat center in some idyllic location removed from the burdens of daily life. Nor is she surrounded with the consoling presence of friends and family. A retreat, especially in an idyllic location, and being surrounded by family and friends are often two situations in life that make it easier for us to perceive the presence and action of God in our life and make it easier for us to believe. They are, most often, moments of consolation for us. That is not Mary's real-life situation at all. Mary is simply listening deeply to the events and circumstances of her life as they really are. This is Mary's "secret," or what I like to call the Marian posture.

The Marian posture is first and foremost a deep and attentive listening to God. This listening says, "Here I am, Lord, with all of myself, just simply before you. I desire only you." It is this posture that enables Mary to ponder, not how crazy life is, but how wonderful and mysterious God is. Also, this posture allows her to experience once again, that even amidst what can appear as crazy, God not only is present but is doing beautiful and profound things. Since Mary is before God like this, she is then able to ponder his mysterious ways. This is Mary's posture in prayer and in life, for it is only she who embraces fully the words of St. Paul:

> *O the depths of the riches and wisdom and knowledge of God! How unsearchable are his judgments and how inscrutable his ways! For who has known the mind of the Lord, or who has been his counselor? Or who has given a gift to him that he might be repaid? For from him and through him and to him are all things. To him be glory for ever. Amen.*
> *—Romans 11:33–36*

This Marian posture reminds us of an essential fact about our relationship with God: Prayer and life are not two separate realities. God and life are not two different worlds. This is why the best context for you and me to pray in and live our spiritual life is in our life as it really is. At the monastery where I am chaplain, I often meet with people on retreat. Almost regularly I hear people say something like this: "If I lived here, I would pray so much better and I would be so much holier." They appear somewhat alarmed when I respond almost immediately, "No, you wouldn't." I remind them that retreats are helpful and necessary for us, however they are not our vocation. Whatever our state in life is, married, single, religious or priest, and wherever our vocation is lived, whether in the country or a city, is the best place for us to live our relationship with God, because this is where he has called us to be. By calling us to a specific place and way of life, he also promises us that this is where he will be for us. It is all too easy for us to daydream about how holy we would be or how easy prayer would be if we lived in a monastery or at a retreat center. Mary shows us another way, and this way is revolutionary: our life, as it really is, contains all that is necessary for a life of holiness. The question remains, however: are we listening to God in our life?

Mary can listen deeply to God in life because she listens deeply to God in prayer. The opposite is true as well. Mary can listen deeply to God in prayer because she listens deeply to God in life. We can trace this Marian posture throughout her entire life.

The Annunciation is a moment of deep union with God, which we could describe as a profound contemplative experience of God, and it leads Mary to visit her cousin Elizabeth. Mary listens to the words of Elizabeth, *"Blessed are you among women, and blessed is the fruit of your womb!" (Luke 1:42)*, and this leads her back to prayer, specifically the prayer of praise that is the Magnificat. From this prayer we are led to the birth of Jesus, where Mary abandons herself to God through the real events and circumstances of her life. Now, with the appearance of the shepherds and angels we return to a contemplative posture, where Mary goes inward to ponder all these mysterious things that are occurring.

Mary moves from prayer to life and from life to prayer. The way she prays is the way she lives. The way she loves, believes, and listens in prayer is the way she loves, believes, and listens in life. The author of the book *The Hermitage Within* describes Mary most eloquently in this regard:

> *A contemplative soul if ever there was one, Mary never left the presence of God. . . . She exposed her virgin soul to the*

warming light of God's love, to be permeated by its rays. . . .
Like a mirror . . . undimmed by any shadow, she received God's
image, to reflect it back in adoration and praise.[13]

THE MARIAN POSTURE IN OUR LIFE

The more deeply I live my life with Mary, the more I realize how desperately I need this Marian posture in my life. I need Mary to teach me how to listen to her Son, both in prayer and in life. Of course, I am not the only one who needs this. We all need this Marian posture in our life. The reason is both simple and comical: we spend most of our day talking to ourselves. We talk to ourselves about God, other people, our desires, our plans, about what we are going to do with "our" life, and so many other things. We have conversations with ourselves about the weather, sports, what other people are wearing and what we are going to eat tonight for dinner. Sometimes, we even answer ourselves! For most of us, much of the time, life is a monologue with ourselves.

In this monologue with ourselves, there is a recurring question that we ask. It is the question "What if?" What if this situation doesn't work out the way I intend? What if I get sick? What if this person doesn't understand me? What if I'm not able to do what I want to do or what I think I should do in life? What if I lose my job? What if my boss, friends, or family members don't recognize the gifts that I have? There is an endless amount of "what ifs" in life. Of course, some of these "what ifs" are not only legitimate, but they would also be prudent and responsible for us to consider to some degree. However, in my own experience, and after I have listened to so many people as a priest, it appears to be a tendency within human nature to become obsessed with such questions rather quickly.

If we live our lives based upon the "what ifs" we become slaves to what might happen, rather than living as free sons and daughters of God. *"If the Son makes you free,"* Jesus tells us, *"you will be free indeed" (John 8:36).* He also reminds us, *"Do not be anxious about your life, what you shall eat or what you shall drink, nor about your body, what you shall put on."* Why? Because *"Your heavenly Father knows that you need them all" (Matthew 6:25, 32).* Mary perfectly embodies her Son's teachings, and her Marian posture is the proof. Despite all the "what ifs" that could have occurred in Mary's life, she always rooted herself in the truth that the presence of God is reality. Even if all of these "what ifs" came true, and the vast majority of them do not, they could not take away God's presence and his love for us. With such confidence and assurance in God, Mary can listen deeply to her life and not get swept away in an emotional frenzy about what could happen.

Without a deep listening to God and prayerfully pondering his presence in the events of our life, we experience a tremendous amount of insecurity. We begin to think, "I must protect myself; I must save my life, I must figure out what to do." Why? "Because life and other people are out to get me. If I don't take control of my life, nothing will happen," or so we think. Of course, I am not advocating becoming passive or indifferent to life, but rather returning to a deeper listening to God. In other words, we need to foster this Marian posture before all of life, whether we are in prayer or at work, whether we are in solitude or surrounded by people, whether we are experiencing consolation or desolation.

CONCLUSION

For Mary, God was not a problem to be solved, but a mystery to be embraced. How did she approach the mystery that is God? With reverence and humility, and most of all, with a listening heart. Though there are several reasons for this I will briefly mention two.

First, God is always greater than we are. He is always more than we can understand or comprehend. He never follows our ways, our ideas, and our plans. Thank God! If God did follow our ways and could be fully comprehended by us, it would not be God that we are following and seeking, but ourselves. In the book of Job, after spending 37 chapters listening to Job and his friends trying to articulate why he is suffering so much, God finally intervenes.

> *Who is this that darkens counsel by words without knowledge?*
> *. . . Where were you when I laid the foundation of the earth? Tell*
> *me, if you have understanding. . . . Have you commanded the*
> *morning since your days began and caused the dawn to know*
> *its place? . . . Have you entered into the springs of the sea or*
> *walked in the recesses of the deep? Have the gates of death been*
> *revealed to you, or have you seen the gates of deep darkness?*
> *—Job 38:2, 4, 12, 16–17*

When God finishes speaking three chapters later, we are told that Job puts his hand over his mouth and repents (Job 40:4, 42:6). God is reminding Job and his friends that he is always much greater than they, and therefore, much greater than they will ever be able to comprehend.

Second, God is always at work and present in every moment, in every situation, in every circumstance and in every person. Often when people say to me, "I feel like God has abandoned me," I always ask them, "Where do you think he went?" My question usually brings a smile to their face, because it reveals to them what is obvious: God can never leave us. What they are expressing is the feeling of being abandoned by God, a feeling that everyone has had and most likely will experience again in the future. That reality, thankfully, is not possible. Therefore, if we desire depth and intimacy with God, we must practice this deep listening and say with Mary, "Here I am, Lord, with all of myself, just simply before you. I desire only you."

When we can say that more regularly and more sincerely, we will know that this Marian posture is beginning to take root in us, and the Kingdom of God is not far behind.

6

The Magi

Union with Mary

*"When they saw the star, they rejoiced
exceedingly with great joy; and going into
the house they saw the child with Mary
his mother, and they fell down and
worshiped him."*
—Matthew 2:10–11

MODERN PERSON SEARCHING FOR DEPTH

E ven though society at large is becoming more secular and fewer people are attending church and practicing organized religion, there is an increasing interest in things like contemplative prayer and mysticism, in fact, in the life of contemplation in general. If you search articles and books written in the past twenty years or so, the word *contemplation* occurs probably more now than in any period of history. This, I believe, is a grace from God.

Contemplation, or contemplative prayer, can be summed up in one word: intimacy. A contemplative is not necessarily a cloistered monk or nun, but a disciple of Jesus who is growing in love. The saints and doctors of the Church throughout the centuries teach us that to grow in greater love for God, there are a few necessities for our spiritual life. These include daily prayer, frequent use of the sacraments, growing in virtue, and an overall generosity in living the gospel in every aspect of one's life. Contemplatives are not necessarily saints; however, they desire to be one, not for their own glory, but simply because saints give God the greatest glory because they love God more. Hence, the fact that more people are writing and speaking about contemplation implies a growing desire among people for depth and intimacy in their relationship with God. This is good news!

During my twenty years as a Franciscan I have read, listened to, and even participated in, this contemporary conversation regarding contemplation. What I have experienced from many people interested in contemplation is humility, sincerity, and a genuine desire for God. However, I believe there are a few things missing. In this conversation, there is great emphasis on things like prayer practices, personal experiences, posture, and breathing. None of these things are irrelevant in our relationship with God, yet none of them are equivalent to, or the cause of, contemplation and mysticism. Even though our experiences, postures, and ways of prayer are important, they are not the cause in and of themselves of greater intimacy with God.

What I perceive to be missing most from this conversation is Mary, or what I would like to refer to in this reflection as "union with Mary." Mary possesses the greatest intimacy with Jesus. No creature has loved or ever will love Jesus or know him better than Mary, the one who bore him in her womb and spent 30 years with him in the ordinary events of daily life.

Mary is, after the sacraments, the place where we find Jesus not only most frequently, but without distortion. Jesus, in Mary, is the Incarnate Son of God. In her there is no heresy, New Age caricature, or modernist reduction of the words, miracles, and person of Jesus Christ. In Mary, Jesus Christ is Lord, and we who are longing for greater intimacy with him can find nobody better than Mary to help us and show us the way of greater union with him.

This is apparent in the Gospel account of the Magi. St. Matthew records that when the Magi *"saw the star, they rejoiced exceedingly with great joy; and going into the house* **they saw the child with Mary his mother,** *and they fell down and worshiped him"* (Matthew 2:10–11, emphasis added). Why is "union with Mary" important and conducive to a life of deepening prayer and intimacy with God? Because wherever Mary is, Jesus is there. *"They saw the child with Mary his mother."* This is what every person has experienced and is experiencing and will experience when we turn to Mary. The Magi experienced this, as did the shepherds, and Elizabeth at the Visitation, and Simeon and Anna in the temple, and so many others. Where did they find Jesus? With Mary his Mother.

HOLY SLAVERY

In his book *The Secret of Mary* St. Louis de Montfort says there are three levels of devotion or relationship that one can have with Mary.

The first level, he says, is basic spirituality. In this level, a person fulfills the duties of his Christian state, he avoids all mortal sin, and he prays to Mary occasionally and honors her as the Mother of God. To people in the world, a person in this first level may appear good and even holy, yet for true holiness to be present there is an essential element lacking. What is lacking is a deep personal love for Mary and an awareness of how important she is for one's relationship with God. In this first level, Mary is merely in the background.

The second level, de Montfort believes, is where most Catholics are. In this level, one begins to have a deeper confidence in and esteem, love, and veneration for Mary. One develops a personal love for her. One prays the Rosary, venerates her pictures and shrines, and makes her known to others. The testimony of the saints from all ages regarding Mary and her importance in one's life begins to move from one's head to one's heart. This level of devotion keeps one from sin, and therefore it is good, holy, and praiseworthy, but it is not yet perfect.

The third level, de Montfort believes, is the most perfect and the one we should all be striving for. In the third level, one surrenders himself in the manner of a slave to Mary, and to Jesus through her, and one attempts to perform all his actions with Mary, in Mary, through Mary, and for Mary. This is what he refers to as holy slavery. This slavery, of course, consists of love and free choice, where one willingly gives himself to her. The inspiration for this level is none other than Jesus himself, who gave himself to us through Mary.

I must admit, when I first read St. Louis de Montfort's description of these various levels of devotion to Mary, I was both intrigued and perplexed. I was intrigued because, even though I always considered my relationship with Mary to be good, which meant that I was in the second level, I also intuited that something was missing. When I would read about saints like Padre Pio, Maximilian Kolbe, Mother Teresa, and so many others, I saw that their Marian devotion appeared to be both the strength and cause for their profound lives of prayer and service. I also realized that among the priests and religious I knew, those who had a deep love for Mary were noticeably different in almost every aspect of life. As I observed this in them and in the saints, my heart simply cried out, "I want what they have." What they had, of course, was Mary, in a deeper and more profound way than I did.

I was perplexed because, like many people, I had to ask myself, "Is this too much? Am I giving too much attention on Mary? Where is the biblical proof for this teaching?" I have heard some people criticize the teaching of St. Louis de Montfort by claiming that his Marian love and devotion is excessive, that for all intents and purposes he meant well, but his would not be considered mature spirituality. "Is this true?" I asked myself. Unfortunately, I will admit, for a period in my life, I assumed it was, and I dismissed his teaching as overly pious. However, what convinced me of the truth and beauty of St. Louis de Montfort's teaching was a closer examination and reflection upon St. John's account of the Crucifixion. In his Gospel, St. John recounts one of the last actions and words of Jesus thus: *"Then he said to the disciple, 'Behold, your mother!' And from that hour the disciple took her to his own home"* (John 19:27).

After the death of Jesus, John took Mary home to live with him. What must that have been like personally for St. John? Was Mary a burden to him? Did St. John ignore her or consider her irrelevant in his life? Did he care for her simply because this is what Jesus asked of him? Did she get in the way of his relationship with Jesus?

The answer to all these questions is no. Rather, St. John now began to live his life with Mary, through Mary, and for Mary. What was the fruit of that relationship? It was the very Gospel that he would write. The Gospel of St. John is, without any doubt, the most profound theological and spiritual work ever written in human history. Many scholars and theologians have devoted their entire lives to studying this Gospel and, after many years of research and study, have only began to scratch the surface of this theological and spiritual masterpiece.

How did St. John write such a profound Gospel, especially since he was not a theologian or a writer? The answer is simple; he was living with Mary. Every day he served her, spoke with her, listened to her, and did whatever she told him to do. He gave himself completely in love and devotion to Mary, and what did she give him in return? Jesus. She gave him a deeper knowledge of Jesus, a deeper understanding of Jesus, and a deeper love for Jesus. Every day as he lived his life with Mary, he saw what a true disciple of Jesus looks like. She became the model and the way in which he would grow in holiness.

St. Louis de Montfort writes,

> As Mary is everywhere the fruitful Virgin, she produces in the depths of the soul where she dwells a purity of heart and body, a singleness of intention and purpose, and a fruitfulness in good works. Do not think that Mary, the most fruitful of all God's creatures, who went as far as to give birth to a God-man, remains idle in a docile soul. She causes Jesus to live continuously in that soul and that soul to live in continuous union with Jesus.[14]

Many people, at some point in their spiritual journey, have officially consecrated themselves to Mary through various means. Perhaps the most popular is St. Louis de Montfort's 33-day consecration program; however, his is not the only one. St. Maximilian Kolbe has a 9-day consecration to Mary program, and a modern version of both is summarized beautifully in the book *33 Days to Morning Glory* by Fr. Michael E. Gaitley.[15] Regardless of which version we use, officially consecrating oneself to Mary can be, as it was for me, a significant moment in one's spiritual life.

However, this total consecration to Mary is not meant to merely be a moment in our spiritual life, nor is it meant to be something we check off our "spiritual to-do list" and conclude that nothing else is necessary. Total consecration, or union with Mary, is not an event in our spiritual life, it is our spiritual life.

When we consecrate ourselves totally to Mary, not only are we following in the footsteps of St. John, St. Louis de Montfort, St. Maximilian Kolbe, and so many other great saints, but we are following in the footsteps of Jesus, who gave himself totally to Mary. We are simply doing what God has done. In the words of Venerable Fr. Gabriel M. Allegra, *"For me the spiritual life is the simplest thing in this world: it consists solely in living with Our Lady, like Jesus."*[16]

UNION WITH MARY IS IMITATION OF JESUS

To illustrate this more clearly, there are many examples we could use. However, I will limit myself to three. First, out of love for Mary, God gave her special privileges, namely her Divine Motherhood, her Immaculate Conception, and her Assumption (and many more). God created Mary free of any imperfection, most pure, full of grace, and therefore holier than all the angels and saints. Mary's Immaculate Conception was not a privilege given to her merely for her own sake, but rather it was ordered toward another privilege, for her to become the Mother of God. Since Mary is Immaculately conceived, and she is the Mother of God who always loved and served her Son, it should be no surprise that Mary would experience another privilege: her Assumption into heaven after her earthly life was finished. She, through the grace and merits of her Son's passion, death, and resurrection, had already been glorified in her body, along with Jesus before the end of time. Truly the mystery of God's privileges in Mary exceeds the limits of our finite minds, as St. Proclus proclaims: *"O man, run through all creation with your thought, and see if there exists anything comparable to or greater than the holy Virgin, Mother of God."* Could these privileges Mary have occurred if God had not given himself fully to her? The answer, of course, is no.

Second, in the Gospel of John we hear that *"God so loved the world that he gave his only-begotten Son . . . not to condemn the world, but that the world might be saved through him"* (John 3:16–17). Jesus comes to this world out of love for humanity, yet he spends most of his time on earth alone with his Mother. We cherish and meditate on the words of Jesus that are recorded in the Gospel, yet Mary was privileged to listen to him speak every day. We are told in the Gospel that at the sight of Jesus, many people would come rushing toward him just to be near him or to have him touch them as he passed by (see Matthew 9:21), yet Mary lived each day in close proximity to Jesus. In the thirty-three years of Our Lord's life here on earth, thirty of those years he gave to Mary his Mother, and three to the rest of humanity. Bishop Fulton Sheen captures this most poignantly when he writes: *"Our Lord spent three hours in redeeming, three years in teaching, and thirty years in obeying."*[17] The point here is obvious: Jesus gave himself totally to Mary, more than to anyone else.

Finally, in contemporary society the Ten Commandments are often portrayed as merely old-fashioned, rigid, moralistic laws. For Jesus, though, the Ten Commandments were a way to love and honor the Father, who is love. He embraced all the commandments with great love and devotion. This includes, of course, the fourth commandment, to honor his father and mother. By honoring his mother, Jesus was obedient to her, hence he gave himself totally to her. After Jesus was found by Joseph and Mary in the temple, we are told that Jesus *"went down with them and came to Nazareth and was obedient to them"* (Luke 2:51).

What is the point of mentioning all of this? It's to show that Jesus did not hesitate to give himself totally to Mary. How then could we do anything different? Why would we want to do anything other than what God has done? What are we waiting for?

PRACTICAL SUGGESTIONS

The most important question for us, then, is how do we live this in real life? Union with Mary looks different for each person. In my own life, it looks like this. Each morning, shortly after I wake up, I begin a time of prayer where I offer everything to Mary. I say something like this: "I place myself totally in your hands, Mary. Let me be your instrument for the glory of God." Then I offer to Mary what I consider the "Big 3": my priesthood, my religious vows, and my will, all for the glory of God. I also offer to her my plans, hopes, and desires for this new day and ask her to use them all for the fulfillment of God's will in my life. Then, I simply renew this prayer throughout the day. Before each activity, before each time of prayer, I attempt to invite Mary to be with me and I speak with her in free moments throughout my day. For example, before a time of prayer I will say to her, "Teach me, Mary, how to pray and be with me, Mary, during this time of prayer." If I have a difficult conversation or task ahead of me I simply ask her, "Please, Mary, be with me in this difficult conversation or in this difficult task. Help me to listen, respond, and work as you would." In free moments throughout the day when I may be outside taking a walk or driving to a store, I will take this opportunity to just speak with her from my own heart.

In short, union with Mary means never doing anything without her. Union with Mary is not time-consuming or emotionally draining, though it does involve inviting her more deeply into our life. It entails a greater awareness of her motherly presence and the desire to imitate Jesus more deeply by living our life completely with Mary, as he did. She, like God, is always present to us. She, like God, and like us, wants to be invited. Neither she nor God will force their presence upon us, and so the task involved in a life of deepening union with Mary is for us to open our heart more fully to her.

This is one of the most powerful and beautiful things we can do in our relationship with God. As we invite Mary more completely into our lives and give ourselves more fully to her, we will encounter God more deeply than we ever could by ourselves. The experience of the Magi and so many others will be ours as well: whenever we see the child it will always be with Mary his Mother. Let us then not be afraid to give ourselves more deeply to his Mother, so that we can know and love her Child even more.

7

The Presentation

Living the Paschal Mystery

"A sword will pierce through your own soul
also, that thoughts out of many
hearts may be revealed."
—Luke 2:33

We are invited into the Paschal Mystery

The priesthood is an awesome responsibility. Essentially, priests are called to direct people's souls to heaven. They are expected to have answers to people's problems, insights into how to live, and clarity regarding God's will. This occurs in everything in life from the most serious to the most mundane. There is no part in people's lives where a priest is irrelevant. Before I was ordained a deacon in 2010, the grave responsibility inherent in the priesthood was, for me, mostly abstract. However, when I was ordained a deacon and began to be more involved in ministry, I soon realized how awesome this vocation was that I was receiving. Along with this awareness came a deep sense of gratitude, but also anxiety. Despite many years of theological training and life as a Franciscan, I felt inadequate and unable to really help people. I was 32 years old when I was ordained a priest, and I thought to myself, "What do I know about God? What do I know about life? I'm only 32 years old!"

Immediately after ordination I began to listen to many people's struggles and problems. In spite of my sincere attempts to solve their problems, I felt my efforts were in vain. There was never a simple solution or an easy answer to the many and varied problems I would encounter. Every person, circumstance, and problem was different and unique. I remember one day after being a priest for only two months, I went into my room and frantically reviewed my notes from the seminary, thinking that the answers must be in there somewhere. Of course, they were not.

During the Easter season of my first year as a priest, I stayed in the chapel one night after night prayer and gazed silently at the crucifix. Suddenly, it hit me: Our life is not a problem, nor is it something we must figure out. This epiphany quickly led to another: God was not asking me to solve everyone's problems.

I realized in that moment the only way our life makes sense is when it is lived through the Paschal Mystery: the suffering, death, and resurrection of Jesus Christ. The Paschal Mystery then is the only adequate reference point we have for life. This does not imply of course that we ignore things like psychology, human development, or the social sciences, but that ultimately the truth about us and God's desire for our life is beyond those things.

Instead of asking "Where is God?" in my own struggles and in those of the people whom God was sending me, I began to perceive a deeper truth beneath what I was experiencing in my own humanity. This truth is that God is inviting us, with our humanity and our life as it really is, to live more deeply his Paschal Mystery. It was no longer I nor these many people I was now encountering as a priest who were suffering. Rather, it was Jesus suffering in them and through them. I wish I could say that once I realized this and experienced this in my own life, it was consoling, and that I never struggled or suffered anymore. It was and it continues to be piercing, confusing, and painful. Yes, the Paschal Mystery contains the Resurrection, but only after the Passion and death.

This truth is brought to light more deeply when Simeon, upon seeing the child Jesus in the temple, addresses these mysterious words to Mary: *"Behold, this child is set for the fall and rising of many in Israel, and for a sign that is spoken against (and a sword will pierce through you own soul also), that thoughts out of many hearts may be revealed"* (Luke 2:34–35).

What is Simeon saying to Mary? He is telling her that she, like all of us, and as the first among us, can live only in and through the Paschal Mystery of her Son. Simeon is also reminding her that she, the Mother of God, has a unique and profound role in that Paschal Mystery. She, therefore, cannot be a passive observer in the life of her Son, and neither can we. *The Catechism of the Catholic Church* addresses this point:

In his incarnate divine person, he has in some way united himself to every man, "the possibility of being made partners, in a way known to God, in the paschal mystery. . . ." This is achieved supremely in the case of his mother, who was associated more intimately than any other person in the mystery of his redemptive suffering. —CCC 618

Mary's Unique Role in the Paschal Mystery

St. John Paul II in his encyclical letter *"Mother of the Redeemer"* offers many rich insights into Mary's role in the Paschal Mystery. The prophecy of Simeon, according to John Paul II, is like a second Annunciation to Mary since it reveals to her the nature and destiny of her Son, who is the Messiah. Specifically, it reveals her Son's mission as Messiah and Savior will be accomplished, but only in misunderstanding and sorrow. He, the suffering servant, will be *"despised and rejected by men; a man of sorrows, and acquainted with grief; and as one from whom men hide their faces"* (Isaiah 53:3). This prophecy reveals ultimately what the response of humanity at large will be to the good news of the Gospel, which is not acceptance, but rejection. Even though the Gospel is the good news of God's love for us, this prophecy reveals the bad news of humanity's response, namely that when God comes to us in Jesus, we will reject him and have him put to death.

Furthermore, St. John Paul II says that Simeon's words confirm Mary's faith in the saving mission of her Son (she never doubts who Jesus is), and this prophecy, though mixed with sorrow, affirms her belief that he is indeed both Messiah and Savior. However, they also reveal to her that her life will also include suffering. She is, as mother and disciple, intimately linked to the Paschal Mystery. His suffering will become her suffering. His sorrows will become her sorrows. Therefore, her motherhood will be tainted with sorrow. In a private revelation to St. Bridget, Mary made this fact known when she said to her, *"As often as I looked at my Son, as often as I wrapped Him in His swaddling clothes, as often as I saw His hands and feet, so often was my soul absorbed, so to say, in fresh grief, for I thought how He would be crucified."*[18]

We can experience, I believe, the depth and beauty of these truths more acutely by first reflecting on them from a merely human and biological level. Over the years in speaking with so many mothers, I have realized that most of the pain and suffering they experience in life is related to the pain and suffering of their children. Mothers, of course, have their own individual suffering, but most of the suffering I have heard from them in my life as a priest is related to the suffering of their children. Regardless of how old their children are or how far away they live, whenever a child suffers, the mother suffers also. If the child is anxious, the mother is anxious. If the child is sad, the mother is sad. If the child is suffering physically, oddly enough, the mother tends to suffer physically in some way as well.

Several years ago, my nephew began having minor seizures at the age of 19. After many doctor visits and tests, there was no solution in sight, and after he began having a seizure almost weekly, this began to take its toll physically on my sister. When she went for her annual physical, it was discovered that she had high blood pressure, something she had never experienced in her life until that moment. When she told me this news, I immediately saw the correlation. Perhaps her high blood pressure was merely a coincidence. However, what I have witnessed regarding the intimate bond between mother and child leads me to another conclusion: my nephew's suffering had become her suffering.

Mary's role, then, as Mother of God is not one of passivity. She does not merely give birth to Jesus and then disappear. Rather, she is called to walk with her Son through the entirety of his Paschal Mystery, a mystery that because it includes suffering for Jesus, will include suffering for Mary. Herein lies the deeply profound and beautiful reality underlying this mysterious prophecy: through Mary's own suffering, she can participate in the saving mission of her Son, the Messiah and Savior. In other words, she can participate in the salvation of the world and fulfill those puzzling words of St. Paul, *"I rejoice in my sufferings for your sake, and in my flesh I complete what is lacking in Christ's afflictions for the sake of his body, that is, the Church" (Colossians 1:24)*. Every moment in her life then is filled with meaning, even while she is suffering.

It is important both to understand more deeply Mary's role and to contemplate her own magnificence more greatly, to reflect on what specifically this suffering is for Mary. First, Mary is told her Son will suffer and die. There is perhaps no greater suffering in this life than when a parent suffers the death of a child. However, there is more occurring for Mary here. Mary is the only Mother whose Son created her; therefore, she is a Mother who must watch both her Son and her God be persecuted, abandoned, and killed. When a mother's child is suffering or is killed, she can turn to God in her pain and devastation, but when Mary's Son, who is God, is suffering and killed, to whom can she turn? This is a whole level of suffering that none of us, thankfully, are aware of. This level of suffering accompanies Mary throughout her entire life, not, as we may think, only during the Passion. Every time Jesus is rejected, which occurs frequently, Mary's heart will be pierced. It is her Son and her God who is being rejected. This suffering, of course, culminates on Calvary, when he, her Son and her God, is crucified and dies.

OUR PARTICIPATION IN THE PASCHAL MYSTERY

Mary's role in the Paschal Mystery is certainly unique; however, it is not entirely remote from us. Let us return to those puzzling words of St. Paul, *"I rejoice in my sufferings for your sake, and in my flesh I complete what is lacking in Christ's afflictions for the sake of his body, that is, the Church"* (Colossians 1:24). These words are deeply mysterious, and, I must admit, the first time I read them I thought it was a misprint or I was reading a poor translation of the text. What could possibly be lacking in the sufferings of Christ, I asked myself? Over time, and through a deeper meditation on Mary, I began to realize there is something lacking in the sufferings of Christ; namely our participation in them.

St. Paul is reminding us that the Paschal Mystery is the mystery of our lives, and that every moment of our lives is meant to be a willing participation in it. This means our life as it really is; even the sufferings and sorrows we experience, have a redemptive value to them. St. Paul can speak about what is lacking in the sufferings of Christ because he is still living while he writes these words, that is, he is still participating in the Paschal Mystery with his life. We too, while we are alive, are still participating in the Paschal Mystery.

Imagine for a moment how beautiful and profound it would be to say with St. Paul, and certainly as Mary did before him, *"I rejoice in my sufferings . . . and **in my flesh I** complete what is lacking in Christ's afflictions. . . ."* Personally, I rarely ever think, act, or speak like this. Instead, my sufferings often lead me to doubt God's presence and love. Once that occurs, my whole interior state, including my thoughts, emotions, and feelings, are covered in darkness and negativity, and before I realize it, I feel as if I am drowning in a pool of desolation. Considering then the immense fruit of Mary's life and St. Paul's, how different would life be if we viewed it like them, only through the Paschal Mystery? If we saw our struggles, the challenges of life, our vocations, and all the mysterious things we encounter in this life as a participation in the Paschal Mystery.

Instead of proclaiming the words of St. Paul and following the example of Mary, I have witnessed both in myself and in others a tendency to view our life as a problem that needs immediate fixing. How often have we thought or said things like, "If only the circumstances or the people in my life were different, then I would be different." So often we view the external realities of our life, people, circumstances, and situations as part of the problems in our life that prevent us from experiencing the life we believe we deserve. Until these problems are removed, we tend to believe, we will not be at peace. Therefore, I cannot pray unless my neighbor turns down his stereo. I cannot forgive this person until he asks for forgiveness. I cannot volunteer at the soup kitchen until all my personal needs are met, and so on. The tragedy in this attitude is that if we wait for our lives to be perfect, we will never do anything in life, simply because life in this world is imbued with imperfections.

Of course, I am not saying we should ignore our problems or not seek to remedy difficult situations. That would be foolish. What I am saying, along with St. Paul and the example of Mary, is that there is a greater reality at work here. Yes, we seek the help we need in this life, whether it is psychological, physical, financial, etc., but those solutions are not the end, they are part of a much larger reality. This larger reality is the Paschal Mystery in our lives. Saying yes to it, as we witness in Mary, can bear tremendous fruit both for ourselves and the world. In fact, there is nothing greater we can do with our lives than this.

CONCLUSION

I have been a priest now for twelve years. In that time, I have heard and experienced things I could never have imagined. In my ministry, there have been moments of great joy, but also great sorrow. There have been moments of deep clarity and confidence, but also moments of great darkness and confusion. There have been moments when God's presence was tangible and consoling, but there have also been moments when God felt far away, and I felt discouraged. Ultimately, there is no amount of seminary training or study that could have prepared me for my life as a priest.

Though I experienced a great deal of anxiety in my first year as a priest regarding how I would help people, thankfully, that anxiety has disappeared almost completely. How did this happen? It is not because I have acquired some special knowledge or wisdom somewhere or have become accustomed to suffering in life. Rather, the more I live my life with Mary, the more she helps me to see and hear Jesus, not only in my life, but in all those I am called to minister to as a priest. What I see him doing and hear him saying in all of us is the same. He is inviting us more deeply into his Paschal Mystery, a mystery that includes suffering and death, but ultimately includes resurrection. The assurance of this can be found in Jesus's own words: *"Unless a grain of wheat falls into the earth and dies, it remains alone; but if it dies, it bears much fruit"* (John 12:24).

What then, if anything, would Mary want to say to us regarding all that has been mentioned here so far? I believe her message would be very simple: do not be afraid of your life. Yes, your life will include suffering. Yes, people in your life will hurt you and disappoint you. Yes, your life will never be what you think it should be or how you may want it to be. However, do not be afraid. Why? Because God is near, so near in fact that he desires for you to share your sufferings and trials with him, so that you and I, like Mary, can participate in the salvation of the world. We must not be afraid, then, to live our lives with all their difficulties, sufferings, and crosses, because all those things are part of the beautiful and mysterious reality that is the Paschal Mystery, which is the mystery of our lives.

8

The Flight into Egypt

Deeper Gift of Self

"Rise, take the child and his mother, and flee
to Egypt, and remain there till I tell you; for
Herod is about to search for the child,
to destroy him."
—Matthew 2:13

FOLLOWING JESUS EQUALS PERSECUTION

I graduated from college in May 2002. A few months later, on September 8, the Feast of the Birth of Mary, I entered the Franciscan Friars of the Renewal at the age of twenty-three. Regarding my decision not to pursue a career, family, or any material gains, I could not have been more blessed. My family was loving and supportive, and the parish I grew up in was the same. My pastor, a very joyful diocesan priest, was like my own personal cheerleader, always encouraging me and offering support whenever I needed it.

When I moved to New York City to join the Franciscans, I thought that support would continue. In fact, I couldn't imagine a life without such support. I was shocked to discover that this was not true for some of my classmates. During my first day as a Franciscan, I was filled with horror when one of my classmates, a 35-year-old businessman, told me his family had disowned him because of his decision to leave their business and respond to God's invitation to become a Franciscan. Another one of my classmates, a 23-year-old graduate student, told me that before he boarded his plane for New York City, his parents caused such a commotion at the airport by crying and begging him not to leave, that the police were called and threatened his parents with arrest if they did not let their son board the plane. Even though my classmates had experienced suffering, persecution, and trials because of the Gospel, I couldn't conceive of such things for myself.

During my first week as a Franciscan, one of my classmates and I decided to go for a walk one night after dinner. It was a warm summer night, and there were hundreds of people scurrying around Broadway. Suddenly, in the middle of our conversation, my classmate and I looked up and were startled to see a woman wearing a leather jacket and covered in tattoos, walking toward us. As she approached me, she stopped, spat in my face, uttered a few curse words, and continued walking. After I wiped the spit off my face, my classmate and I looked at each other in amazement, and decided it was time to return to the friary to say night prayer.

Several days later, all of us new Franciscans were praying outside an abortion clinic in Manhattan when suddenly a man came out of the clinic, walked over to us, and broke a bottle on a fire hydrant located directly in front of me. He too uttered a few curse words at us before leaving. Luckily, none of the glass got into my eye, but I did receive several cuts on my hands and feet. After both incidents I remember sitting in the chapel back at the friary and thinking, "Why didn't these people like me? I wasn't rude. I didn't say anything offensive, and I didn't even know these people. Didn't they know that as a Franciscan I was there to help people?

The following week during Mass, I heard Jesus say these words in the Gospel: *"If the world hates you, know that it has hated me before it hated you. If you were of the world, the world would love its own; but because you are not of the world, but I chose you out of the world, therefore the world hates you"* (John 15:18–19). Immediately it hit me: I no longer belonged to the world because Jesus had chosen me out of the world. When these people saw me, especially in my religious habit and praying, it was Jesus they were spitting on or trying to intimidate. It was Jesus whom they hated, and I was being invited to experience the persecution and suffering that he encountered his entire life.

As we begin now to reflect on the next episode in Mary's life, the flight into Egypt, let us consider these words from the Catechism of the Catholic Church: *"The flight into Egypt (and the massacre of the innocents) make manifest the opposition of darkness to the light. . . . Christ's whole life was lived under the sign of persecution. . . . **His own share it with him**"* (CCC 530, emphasis added).

Persecution is the normal experience, to varying degrees, of a disciple of Christ. *"A servant is not greater than his master. If they persecuted me, they will persecute you" (John 15:20)*. Long before I or you or the martyrs would experience persecution for Christ, Mary was the first to share in this opposition to the light, hence she was the first to experience persecution for the sake of Christ. Herod, because he went after Christ, went after Mary, because as we have mentioned already, wherever he is, she is.

A DEEPER GIFT OF SELF

Until now, Mary's life has been relatively calm, at least exteriorly. We have reflected on her marveling at the presence of her Son, and marveling at the ways in which he has been made known to her. This has occurred through various means: the words of the angel Gabriel and of Mary's cousin Elizabeth, the circumstances of Jesus's birth in Bethlehem, and the presence of the shepherds and Magi. In all these occurrences there has been a deeply receptive and contemplative experience of God for Mary. But now, with the flight into Egypt, her posture moves from receiving Jesus to protecting him. This protecting is going to cost Mary (and Joseph) a great deal, because it is going to demand of them a deeper gift of self that neither of them has experienced thus far.

The journey from Bethlehem to Egypt was about 400 miles. It was wintertime, which means that most likely Mary and Joseph had to travel in wintry conditions such as snow, rain, or heavy winds. Mary was fifteen years old, a delicate young woman who was unaccustomed to such journeys. To arrive at Egypt from Bethlehem there were two possible routes, neither of which was easy. One route would take Joseph and Mary along the sand dunes of the Mediterranean coast to Egypt. Another route would take them across the northern part of the Sinai peninsula to the seacoast and into the Delta. Whichever way they chose, the journey was laborious, demanding about two to three weeks of exhausting travel. They would be fortunate if, and only if, they owned a donkey or a camel upon which Mary and the child Jesus could ride at least in intervals.

To us modern people this may sound exciting and adventurous. However, it is important for us to keep in mind that there were no tour guides, flight attendants, or fellow pilgrims to provide comfort and consolation to Mary and Joseph. There was no film crew documenting their experience for a reality TV show, nor was there an abundance of material means to ensure safety and comfort for their travels. All they had, besides each other, was the message of the angel to Joseph to *"rise, take the child . . . and flee to Egypt, and remain there till I tell you" (Matthew 2:13)*.

What was being asked of Mary here? Whether it be persecution, suffering, or simply the difficulties that we experience in life, the same thing was being asked of Mary as it is of us: a deeper gift of self.

DEEPER GIFT OF SELF: THE MAIN INGREDIENT IN GROWTH

Throughout the centuries many spiritual writers have described one's relationship with God as progressing through a series of stages. Dionysius, in the fifth century, was the first to organize the spiritual life into three stages: the purgative, illuminative and unitive ways. This is by far the most popular model that has been used over the centuries when attempting to describe what growth in the spiritual life looks like. As insightful as this model is, it is not the only one. St. Teresa of Avila in the sixteenth century described the soul as a castle, with Jesus at the center. To arrive at the center of this castle, she says, one must pass through various rooms or mansions. Though this may sound easy, St. Teresa reminds us that moving through these various mansions requires not only the grace of God, but extreme generosity on our part. St. John of the Cross described the spiritual life as climbing a mountain, Mount Carmel. As we journey up the mountain, which for St. John entails sufferings, trials, and deep purifications, we become transformed more deeply as our faith, hope, and love mature. Once again, for this maturation to occur, not only is the grace of God necessary, but a deeper gift of self on our part is also necessary.

What all these spiritual authors are attempting to remind us of is that holiness is a continuing journey outward, away from self. It is a journey away from what I merely understand with my rational mind, from what I find comfortable, from what I think, feel, or even want, simply with my own humanity. In short, growing in holiness means moving away from myself as the reference point for everything.

Hence, St. John of the Cross refers to this growth as a dark night, because the further we travel away from self with its limited perceptions, understandings, feelings, and desires, the more deeply we enter into the mystery, transcendence, and incomprehensibility of God. This experience is like a dark night for us, because the closer one comes to God, the more one realizes God is nothing like what we may have imagined or what our senses might have suggested about him. He is infinitely more. What is necessary then, at least on our end, to move more deeply into the mystery of God is not more prayer, penance, or work, though it certainly may include those things, but ultimately a deeper gift of self. Jesus implies this when he says, *"He who loses his life for my sake will find it"* (Matthew 10:39).

This, unfortunately, terrifies us and can paralyze us at times. It is not uncommon that when a person is progressing in the spiritual life he often feels, or may be led to believe, that the opposite is occurring. After all, while walking through a dark night one does not have the same confidence and courage that one may experience in the middle of the day. "If I were really growing in holiness, wouldn't I feel different?" many people say. "If I were really growing in holiness, wouldn't I have some awareness of where I am and what God is doing in my life?" Though these questions are both normal and rational, the surprising answer to all of them is, no, you wouldn't.

The reason for this is simple. Every step deeper with God is a step into the unknown, at least for our senses. We are never given a manual by God that provides a step-by-step instruction regarding every moment of our spiritual life. The reality is, in this next step in our relationship with God, we don't know what it is going to look like or be like. We don't know what we are going to look like or be like. We don't know how we are going to feel or how other people will respond or react to us. Our senses, which for many things in life help us, are now for the most part useless when it comes to growing in intimacy with God. The simple reason for that is that God is much bigger than our sense perception.

St. John of the Cross states: *"The soul is not united with God in this life through understanding, or through enjoyment, or through imagination, or through any other sense; but only faith, hope, and charity can unite the soul with God in this life."*[19]

DEEPER GIFT OF SELF IS ABOUT BEING MORE, NOT DOING MORE

I have noticed, especially among priests and religious, that if someone mentions the phrase "a greater gift of self," there is at least internally a certain amount of anxiety and even anger that wells up within them. The reason for this is not that these priests and religious are not willing to be generous, because in fact most of them are, but it is because we often associate a greater gift of self as being synonymous with more work. In short, we conclude that to give a greater gift of self means that we must work more and harder. Many of the priests and religious that I know work extremely hard and are already overworked. The last thing they need, and this is true for most disciples of Christ, is more responsibilities. Thankfully, though sometimes a greater gift of self results in more work, primarily a greater gift of self is about being more and not doing more.

This, I believe, is abundantly clear in Mary's flight to Egypt. In this event in Mary's life we might ask what work God is calling Mary to complete. The answer is "nothing." Yes, she is instructed to take Jesus and flee to Egypt, but before she can say yes to that work, she must interiorly stand before God with a greater willingness to give him everything. Hence, before she can take the child Jesus and flee to Egypt she must open her heart more deeply to God through a greater trust, surrender, and obedience. Once this greater gift of herself to God occurs interiorly, she can accomplish the work or mission in which God asks her to participate. Her exterior strength or success, that is, her doing, corresponds only the degree of her generosity with God interiorly. St. Maximilian Kolbe reiterates the importance of our being before doing when he writes,

> The fruit of our work does not depend on cleverness, strength, money, even though these things are gifts of God and also useful for apostolic activity; but only and solely on the degree of our union with God. If this is lacking or becomes sluggish, all other contributing factors will not help at all. Rather, if such union with God is strong, we will find all things possible and without difficulty.[20]

A deeper gift of self then is first and foremost a deeper opening of our whole self to God that begins interiorly and then manifests itself exteriorly. Therefore ministry, without the proper interior depth, almost always leads to burnout. If it doesn't lead immediately to burnout, then ministry, without an interior depth, is plagued by things like pride, competition, and jealousy. In other words, one's own ego becomes the focus, instead of sharing the love of God with one's neighbor. Of course, all these human realities will be present to some degree regardless of how deep our interior life is. However, without this movement of a deeper gift of self, our ministry will be nothing more than social work. Social work is a great good, but its primary concern is for the person in this world. Ministry, though deeply concerned with one's life in this world, is ultimately meant to be pointing a person beyond this world, to eternity.

MARY AND THE GIFT OF SELF

In conclusion, then, let us return to Mary. This deeper gift of self is one among many themes that we witness throughout Mary's life. It begins at the Annunciation and continues all the way to the Crucifixion and beyond. Amidst all the joys and sorrows of her life, Mary never holds back anything of herself from God. Even though she never preached to the multitudes, wrote spiritual or theological books, or participated in vast apostolic missions, she was more "successful" and remains so than any missionary or preacher ever was or will be. What is the nature of her "success"? She has given her entire self to God to be used as he desires. This is what God desires of us as well, and it can only occur through a deeper gift of self.

Our need for Mary to help us and assist us with our own deeper gift of self should then be obvious. This gift, as we have been reflecting, is what God is calling us to every moment in life, whether we are experiencing persecution, suffering, or simply the daily struggles each one of us encounters in life. I believe that we cannot do this without her, and God does not want us to attempt this without her.

I spent the first ten years of my religious life trying to follow Christ by myself, with what I would describe as a basic love and devotion to Mary. I wasn't deliberately trying to avoid Mary; however, I was not yet aware of my deep need for her. During this time, I grew in my vocation and my relationship with God. Even though I was sincere in all of this, looking back, I have realized that, as for most of us, my motivation was not perfect. Yes, I wanted to be a good and holy priest; however, I realized that what I was most concerned about during this time was acquiring spiritual knowledge and experience. I was, unfortunately, grasping for consolation and spiritual experiences rather than purely seeking the living God and giving myself more fully to him through a life of genuine faith, hope, and love.

Once I gave myself more fully to Mary, my attitude and therefore my relationship with God changed dramatically. Instead of seeking the things of God for myself and attempting to build a sort of spiritual résumé, I became less interested in acquiring anything, even spiritual experiences, and more concerned with giving everything away, especially myself. In other words, this tremendous grace of making a deeper gift of myself occurred, I am convinced, because of Mary's presence in my life.

After appearing to St. Juan Diego Mary said to him:

> *I am your merciful Mother. . . . Do not be troubled. . . . Am I not here who am your Mother? Are you not under my shadow and protection? Are you not in the folds of my mantle? In the crossing of my arms. Is there anything else you need?*[21]

The answer of course is no, there is nothing else that we need. Mary, and only Mary, can help us make a greater gift of ourselves to God. In many ways, this shouldn't surprise us, since it is simply the natural consequence of being with her, who gave herself continually to God each day.

9

Return from Egypt

An Interior Journey of Faith

*"Rise, take the child and his mother, and go
to the land of Israel, for those who sought the
child's life are dead."*
—*Matthew 2:20*

ORDINARY LIFE AT NAZARETH

My primary ministry as a priest has been that of a spiritual director. Over the years, I have directed hundreds of people on individual retreats, and each month I meet with about 20 people individually for spiritual direction. Both on the retreats and in monthly spiritual direction I have accompanied some of those people through a discernment process, and I continue meeting with them as they begin to live their vocation. This includes couples preparing for marriage, men and women discerning religious life, or people discerning a particular ministry or path in life. After they have discerned God's will for them and have been living it for a few months, when I ask them how they are doing their response tends to be something like this: "The community (or spouse or ministry) is great. I couldn't imagine things to be any better. I'm so happy."

As the months and years go by, their answer to that question—how are they doing—begins to change. Generally, things remain good, but the community, spouse, or ministry they once discerned is no longer the answer to their life that they believed it was. Now there are new questions that demand new answers. What they once discerned no longer has the excitement or the emotional high that it did many years ago. They discover, much to their surprise, that their vocation looks nothing like they once imagined it would.

This stage in one's life is a delicate and important moment. If it is not discerned properly, and without an adequate amount of prayer and reflection, one could and often does walk away from that vocation. When this sort of mini crisis occurs, a natural question arises: did I discern properly? Usually, in my experience, they have. What then has happened in their vocation? They have been led into Nazareth, that is, into ordinary life.

Ordinary life, for the most part is . . . ordinary. Some might even suggest that it is rather boring. Perhaps this could explain why many people try to escape their ordinary life through some alternative means. Think about an ordinary day in your life for a moment. You wake up, pray, go to work, eat a few meals, interact with others, maybe exercise or read a little, and then you repeat basically the same pattern the next day. Occasionally we experience some exciting moments in our daily life. Maybe we meet a friend for lunch whom we haven't seen in a long time. Maybe on the weekend we go to a concert or a sporting event. Maybe we spend a weekend on retreat. These moments, as precious as they are, are few and far between. They are not normal daily occurrences.

Ordinary life then, for most people, is not like an amusement park. While at an amusement park, one moves from one exciting thing to another, whether it be a different roller coaster, a new waterslide, or exotic food and candy. As much as we may desire life to be like this, that's just not how it is for most of us. Rather, life is more like a desert. In a desert, there is little change that occurs, there is not much consolation and stimulus, nor is there usually much excitement that occurs in the desert. Now, some who are reading this may find this outlook bleak and even depressing. Though I do not intend it to be so, life, from what I have observed, is more like a desert than an amusement park.

For many people, this is very difficult to accept. We expect life to be like a movie, filled with excitement, romance, and adventure. When we begin to discover that life is nothing like the way it is portrayed in movies, books, and even social media, this can and often does challenge our faith. It can make us question who God is and cause us to doubt God's presence in our life. Also, it can force us to reexamine our ideas about who we think we are, and what the meaning of our life is. Because ordinary life does this, it is so good for us.

Ordinary life, as I will begin to illustrate through Mary's example, is God's therapy for our exaggerated, unrealistic images and expectations of God, ourselves, and others. Despite its apparent lack of excitement, ordinary life is where our relationship with God thrives, simply because ordinary life is what is most common for us. Pope Paul VI reiterates this point when he writes:

> *Nazareth should teach us how to meditate . . . to reflect on the deeply spiritual, and to be open to the voice of God's inner wisdom. . . . It can teach us the value of study and preparation, of meditation, of a well-ordered personal life, and of silent prayer that is known only to God.*[22]

Mary in Nazareth

Mary's life, up until this point, has been rather full. Angels, her cousin Elizabeth, traveling to Bethlehem, shepherds, Magi, and Herod have all left Mary quite busy, at least exteriorly. Now, as she returns from Egypt to Nazareth a new chapter in her life begins: a chapter where exteriorly, her life will slow down, and she will begin to live ordinary life with St. Joseph and the child Jesus. The Holy Family, at least outwardly, can now begin to live like every other family in first-century Palestine.

This ordinary life will be, in fact, how Mary and Jesus will spend most of their life. Many biblical scholars suggest that the Holy Family spent about three years in Egypt, which would make Jesus three or four years old as they returned to Nazareth. His public ministry lasted only three years, and having died at the age of thirty-three, Jesus thus spent about twenty-five years of his life in Nazareth with Mary, living an ordinary life.

This, I believe, is extraordinary, and something we must marvel at deeply. God not only enters our world, but he also lives and embraces ordinary human life. There are an infinite number of ways in which God could have revealed himself to us, and there are also an infinite number of ways in which God could have redeemed us.

However, let us not forget that God's revelation of himself to us, and our redemption, are both two realities in which God did not have to participate. There is no law that would force God to do any of this. Rather, his revelation and our redemption—and we can also include creation in this—are signs of his love and mercy for us, since none of them are necessities that have forced themselves upon God.

The prologue of St. John's Gospel, perhaps the most profound text in all of Scripture, captures the extraordinary nature of this truth in a single verse: *"The Word became flesh and dwelt among us"* *(John 1:14)*. The phrase "dwelt among us" in Greek means that Jesus "tabernacled" or "pitched his tent" among us. God not only reveals himself but chooses to live among us, and his choice to live among us is a choice to live an ordinary human life. How utterly profound! St. John repeats this truth again in the book of Revelation when he writes, *"Behold, the dwelling of God is with men. He will dwell with them, and they shall be his people, and God himself will be with them"* *(Revelation 21:3)*.

Considering then the astonishing reality of the Incarnation, and the fact that Mary lived each day in the closest proximity to it, we can ask ourselves, what did intimacy with God look like in Nazareth for Mary? What specifically did Mary do with Jesus in Nazareth? What she did with him is so utterly human, and therefore so utterly profound: in Nazareth Mary ate with Jesus, she prayed with him, laughed with him, cried, sat, spoke, listened, and walked with him. In other words, she lived her entire life with him; nothing was excluded, and all of this occurred amid ordinary life.

So often we tend to divide our life into various categories, and the result is not the integration of our one life but the dividing and compartmentalizing of our life into many others. We speak about our spiritual life, our social life, our work life, and our personal life. So many lives we live, or so we think. Mary, I believe, did not think about her life the way we do. For her, there was only life. There was no such thing as a spiritual life, an active life, or a contemplative life. There was just life with Jesus! Sometimes that life was very quiet and peaceful, sometimes it was busy and stressful, sometimes it was fun and exciting, and sometimes it was painful and confusing.

In the movie *The Passion of the Christ*[23] there is a scene that is forever imprinted on my heart. In this scene, Jesus is building a table and a chair, while his mother is preparing supper. Mary comes outside to view her Son's work and tells him that supper is ready. However, before Jesus can come inside, he must wash his hands and take off his work vest. As Mary brings a bowl of water for Jesus to wash his hands, Jesus sprinkles Mary with water in her face, and gives her a big hug and kiss on the cheek. As Jesus is hugging Mary, a beautiful and tender smile appears on Mary's face.

Regardless of how often I have watched this scene, and I have watched it many times, it always brings a tear to my eyes. Why? Because it's the beauty of Nazareth. It's the beauty of ordinary life. It is the beauty that our life can be when it is lived with Jesus and Mary. If an ordinary life is good enough, and not only good enough, but chosen by Jesus and Mary, should it not be good enough for us also? Ordinary life, as we see in Nazareth, is the normal place where we will find God, simply because that is what is most common for us.

LIFE IS AN INTERIOR JOURNEY OF FAITH

There are many implications stemming from this truth. The first, and I believe the most important, is that Nazareth reminds us that the real journey in life is interior. In other words, life is an interior journey of faith. When I graduated from high school, I spent two years traveling throughout the country, because I believed that truth and the meaning of my life were somewhere "out there." I was convinced that by traveling I would discover what I was desperately looking for. Even though I enjoyed that time and considered it a great blessing, it wasn't until I returned home and began to live a more interior life with God that I discovered more deeply truth and the meaning of my life.

In those two years of traveling I drove approximately ten thousand miles, and when I returned home, I was basically the same person, with the same unanswered questions and the same deep yearning in my heart. After three months of being at home and beginning to pray daily, attend Mass, and read the Bible, I received more insight to my questions in that time than during my two previous years on the road. The truth, I discovered, was not "out there," but interior. As Jesus says, *"The kingdom of God is within you"* (Luke 17:21, DRA).

There is much today written and spoken of regarding the importance of living in the present moment. This is necessary, especially considering the fragmented and hectic pace of life that much of modern society is immersed in. However, we must qualify the point here. What we are discussing, and what Mary at Nazareth is attempting to teach us, is not merely to be attentive to the present moment. Rather, Mary is teaching us to live in the present moment of our ordinary life, but to live it with faith ultimately in God's presence and love, which, as we will see, is an active disposition.

At Vatican II, the council fathers, specifically in the document *Dei Verbum*, remind us that faith is our personal response to the Word of God, that is, to the Revelation of God. Faith, the fathers tell us, demands a response of our whole self to what God has revealed. Jesus himself hints at this when he says, *"Why do you call me 'Lord, Lord' and not do what I tell you?"* (Luke 6:46). Despite the increasing amount of conversation today regarding God in books and podcasts and on YouTube, this is only the first step toward genuine Christian faith. As good and as necessary as this conversation is, genuine faith demands more from me than merely talking about it. No matter how many books I read or podcasts I listen to about God, I am not guaranteed faith by any of this. Christian faith demands that my entire life be formed and shaped around the revelation of God, which, as Jesus reminds us, is our only security.

Every one who comes to me and hears my words and does them . . . is like a man building a house, who dug deep, and laid the foundation upon rock; and when a flood arose, the stream broke against that house, and could not shake it, because it had been well built." —Luke 6:47

Specifically, then, this means that my ordinary life, which is most of my life, demands from me a personal response to the truth of God and who he is. Hence, when I'm in the kitchen preparing dinner, or at the doctor's office, or stuck in traffic, or sick at home, all these ordinary moments of life are really means and opportunities to grow in intimacy with God. How do I grow in intimacy with God? Through faith, especially faith amid ordinary life. There is then no circumstance, situation, or experience in life that cannot assist my own growth in the life of faith. Despite how we might feel, our ordinary life is meant to be a help and not a hindrance in our relationship with God.

In St. Paul's letter to the Romans, he speaks about *"the obedience of faith" (Romans 1:5).* This phrase, *the obedience of faith*, is one the council fathers at Vatican II referenced when attempting to portray ultimately what faith is and what it must look like. Mary perfectly embodies this obedience of faith and reveals what faith is and what it should look like. Even though her life in Nazareth with Jesus on the surface was ordinary, her *"obedience of faith"* made it extraordinary. This is how ordinary life can be beautiful. We can be stuck in a traffic jam with Jesus. We can be waiting in a doctor's office with Jesus. We can have a cup of coffee with Jesus. If we live all these moments in this *"obedience of faith,"* like Mary we too will be living an extraordinary life.

If we ever want to know if we are really praying and growing in our relationship with God, 99% of the time the answer to those questions is not revealed to us during times of prayer or spiritual exercises. Rather, it is revealed in the degree in which we live ordinary life: How we treat the people God places in our life. How generous we are with our time and talents. How we react when someone close to us is praised or how we react when someone close to us has fallen or is struggling. In other words, when we live our ordinary life as Mary did, we can be assured that we are growing in holiness, because our faith is genuine. Our life is the proof of that.

CONCLUSION

What then would Mary say to each one of us about our life? I believe she would say these very mysterious words: "Your life is perfect." If I were to say these words to another person, or if another person said those words to me, like most of us I would respond negatively and say something like, "How can you say that? You don't know me or my life. You don't know how I have been treated or what I have suffered. You don't know my past and you don't know what my present situation is like." Of course this is true. Nobody, not even our closest friends, can comprehend all that we have experienced in life. The exception to this is Jesus and Mary. They do know us. They know how we have been treated and what we have suffered. They know our past and what our current life is like. They know our struggles, our pains, and our sorrows, and still I believe Mary would say to us, "Your life is perfect."

By telling us that "our life is perfect" she is not indicating that our life is free of suffering, trials, or heartaches. As she herself knows and experienced, there is no life free of such things. She, who spent three hours undergoing the most intense interior crucifixion while her Son hung on the cross, understands more than anyone the pain and sorrow that is present in life. Mary is not piously glossing over all that we have experienced in life. Rather, she is attempting to show us a much broader perspective about our life. That perspective is merely the fact that our life is perfect for an encounter with God, and that our life, as it really is right now, contains everything you and I need to grow in our relationship with God and respond more deeply to the *obedience of faith* that is asked of us.

Let us then turn more deeply to Mary, who is the perfect embodiment of faith, so that like her, we can live our ordinary life with, in, and through her Son, and therefore turn our ordinary lives into something extraordinary.

10

The Child Jesus in the Temple

The Presence of Jesus

"How is it that you sought me? Did you not know that I must be in my Father's house?"
—Luke 2:49

THE PRESENCE OF JESUS

When I was 20 years old I experienced a life-changing event during a retreat at a Trappist monastery. This experience occurred 23 years ago, yet its memory is so fresh in my mind that it feels as if it just happened yesterday. I was on summer break from college and was visiting Genesee Abbey in upstate New York on a discernment retreat. I had read Thomas Merton a few months earlier, and like many people who read him, I was instantly attracted to the monastic life, and begun to wonder if God was calling me to be a monk.

As I arrived at the monastery, I was still recovering from my own recent reversion back to Catholicism. In all honestly, I had only been a practicing Catholic again for a very short time before I visited the monastery. However, as soon as I returned to the Church, I immediately became aware of my vocation. During this time, I read a biography of St. Charles de Foucauld, who said: *"The moment I realized that God existed, I knew that I could not do otherwise than to live for him alone."* The same was true for me.

The first liturgical office of the day at the monastery is called Vigils, which begins at 3:30 a.m. For forty-five minutes I chanted psalms and listened attentively to various biblical and spiritual texts with the monks, all of which took place in an atmosphere of silence, prayer, and stillness. This new environment, vastly different from the college campus I came from, was a welcome change for me, and it was exactly what my heart had been longing for. During my first 24 hours at the monastery, I fluctuated between gratitude and a deep state of shock because of the simplicity, beauty, and prayerfulness in which these monks lived.

After Vigils on my first morning, I left the monastery and began the five-minute walk to the retreat house where I was staying. The monks had cleared a path through a field so that guests could avoid walking on the road and therefore could maintain a spirit of prayer and silence as they walked back to the retreat house. After walking on this path for a minute or two, I suddenly stopped because I became aware of a presence. This presence was unlike anything I had ever experienced before in my life. It was not another retreatant, it was not one of the monks coming to check on me, it was not an animal walking around in the field, nor was it an image in my own mind. Rather, this presence was gentle, firm, and patient, but also asking something of me, and it was calm and confident. It was completely otherworldly.

This presence, I'm convinced, was Jesus. He did not say or do anything specific. The bush in front did not catch on fire, the ground beneath me did not begin to quake, nor was there heavy thunder and lightning above me. He was just there, without anything spectacular occurring, except of course the tremendous peace and authority that radiated from his presence. It was as if he was revealing himself to me simply to reassure me of all my doubts, fears, and questions. It was a confirmation that he, and he alone, was the answer to my life and the deepest yearnings of my heart. Most importantly, he was telling me, *I am real.*

I did not say anything, nor do I remember thinking anything. My faculties, in retrospect, were paralyzed. I immediately fell to my knees in awe, and within a minute the experience was over. Thankfully, however, its effect would never leave me. I walked back to the retreat center and spent the rest of the retreat in the chapel, looking at Jesus deeply in the Eucharist, on a crucifix, and in the Gospels. If I did step outside for a few moments during that retreat, it was his presence that I began to perceive in nature. I had become, in only a few hours, totally mesmerized by the presence of Jesus.

Writing about this experience is difficult for me, simply because I don't know exactly what happened to me that morning at the monastery. I'm not claiming that I had a vision, or that I experienced a spiritual locution or anything like that. All I know is that I became vividly aware of the presence of Jesus, and by doing so, I realized that nothing else mattered.

MARY, THE CONTEMPLATIVE

The next episode that we will reflect on in Mary's life is, as the fifth joyful mystery of the Rosary names it, the finding of the child Jesus in the temple. This is a mystery, ultimately, regarding the presence of Jesus. Jesus is 12 years old and is accidentally lost while in Jerusalem celebrating the Passover with Mary and Joseph. His parents are understandably worried and anxious, for their son is lost. Finally, after three days they find him. Jesus, however, is not looking for them. He is not anxious. He is not looking to return to Nazareth. Instead, he is in the temple, sitting with the teachers, listening and asking them questions, while everyone is amazed and astonished at his understanding.

Finally, once Mary approaches Jesus, she speaks to him the way any parent would who was worried about their child: *"Son, why have you treated us so? Behold, your father and I have been looking for you anxiously"* (Luke 2:48). To which Jesus responds so calmly, yet so firmly, *"Did you not know that I must be in my Father's house?"* (Luke 2:49). There is no response from Mary, at least that we know of. Rather, we are told that she *"kept all these things in her heart"* (Luke 2:51). This is one of the most revealing lines in Scripture about Mary, as it perfectly summarizes her interior life.

This, of course, is not the first time we hear this about Mary. After the shepherds and angels visited her and the child Jesus in Bethlehem, we are told that *"Mary kept all these things, pondering them in her heart"* (Luke 2:19). At the Presentation after Simeon's prayer of praise we are told that Mary *"marveled at what was said about him"* (Luke 2:33).

What is Mary pondering and keeping in her heart? Ultimately, it is Jesus. More specifically, it is his words, his actions, and his very presence. Hence, she is the perfect model of what a rich and deep interior life looks like, and she becomes for us an icon of what our interior life is meant to look like. Christians from the very early Church recognized in Mary not only a good example by which to be edified, but also the example to follow in our own interior life. Pope Paul VI states this clearly when he writes,

> *Mary is not only an example for the whole Church in the exercise of divine worship but is also, clearly, a teacher of the spiritual life for individual Christians. The faithful at a very early date began to look to Mary and to imitate her in making their lives an act of worship of God and making their worship a commitment of their lives.*[24]

All throughout my life Mary has spoken to me, not audibly of course, but in the quiet recesses of my own heart. Her words to me throughout my life have been encouraging, strengthening, and consoling. However, the most consistent word that Mary has spoken to me is the word *remember*. When I don't know what to do or how to act in a specific situation, she tells me to remember her Son's actions. When I am feeling anxious or incompetent, she tells me to remember his presence in my life. When I don't know what to say or how to understand a situation, another person, or even my own heart, she tells me to remember her Son's words. This word, though so simple, has a powerful effect.

Why does she tell me, and really all of us, to remember? Because so often, without intending for it to be this way, the presence of Jesus gets blurred amid the demands, stresses, and busyness of our daily life. Even if we love Jesus and are seeking to follow him, it is so easy for us forget him. Hence, the need to remember. In Mary's heart there was a constant remembering, a constant pondering and keeping in her heart the words, actions, and presence of her Son. Mary desires that we imitate her in this remembering, not because it brings her glory, but because it roots us more deeply in her Son.

There is much more to this "remembering" than merely recalling a past event. It is not living in the past, but it is living in that one place where God most assuredly is found: the present moment that is today. St. John Paul II reminds us that *"Mary's contemplation is above all a remembering,"* and that *"we need to understand this word in the biblical sense of remembrance (zakar) as a making present of the works brought about by God in the history of salvation."*[25] Through this remembering, St. John Paul II teaches us, the works brought about by God in the history of salvation belong not only to yesterday, but also to today. Hence, even though historically the words and actions of Jesus occurred a long time ago, they are made present to us today, each time we, like Mary, "ponder them in our hearts."

This insight, though deeply beautiful and rich, is not something foreign to the Christian psyche. After all, this is what occurs in the liturgy. Every year we celebrate the seasons of Advent and Christmas, Lent and Easter, and many other feast days. The reason we repeat these celebrations each year is that by recalling these events of salvation history we hope and pray that they can occur more deeply in us. We celebrate Christmas every year not simply to remember that Christ was born a long time ago, but so that Christ can be born again more deeply in us today. We celebrate Lent and Easter each year so that Christ's suffering, death, and resurrection can grow within us and take deeper root within us, so that Christ can be alive and risen in us today.

Not only is this true in the liturgy, but also this is true in the Word of God. The Word of God is a living word. For example, when we hear or read the Beatitudes, we are not merely listening to a sermon that Jesus gave 2,000 years ago. We are also listening to a sermon that Jesus is giving to us as we are listening to or reading the text. When we hear Jesus call Matthew to *"Follow me" (Matthew 9:9)*, we are not merely reflecting on the call of one of Jesus's disciples 2,000 years ago, but we are also hearing that same call addressed to us today in our real-life circumstances.

Mary then, by keeping *"all of these things in her heart,"* reveals to us what mature discipleship looks like. Another name for mature discipleship is the contemplative life. Often, when we speak of the contemplative life, we refer to the life of a cloistered monk or nun. However, we must distinguish between the contemplative life and the contemplative state. The contemplative life is what relationship with God is like after we have progressed a bit in love of God and neighbor, whereas the contemplative state is an exterior form of life that is conducive to a person's leading a contemplative life, usually in a cloister. Hence, the contemplative life is not reserved only for cloistered monks and nuns. Rather, it is God's will for each one of us, since it is the fruit of mature discipleship.

JESUS—THE SOURCE OF TRUE CONTEMPLATION

With all that has been said so far, it is important to state a fact that will be obvious to some, but unfortunately not so obvious to others. The contemplative life has Jesus at the center. To state it even more simply, Jesus *is* the contemplative life. In the Gospel of John, Jesus reminds us, *"I am the way, and the truth, and the life" (John 14:6)*, and *"apart from me you can do nothing" (John 15:5)*. It is inconceivable to imagine growth in holiness if he, who is truth itself and without whom we can do nothing, is not at the center of our life. Without Jesus there is no contemplative life.

This, I believe, is important to emphasize before we can begin to speak more deeply about genuine growth in holiness. In my 20 years as a Franciscan I have visited retreat centers and religious houses, and I have read books where there is an ample amount of discussion on topics such as prayer, spiritual growth, and interior transformation. I have been shocked, and even scandalized at times, to find that in some of this literature and discussion there is hardly any mention of Jesus at all. Recently, someone asked me to read a popular book that was published a few months ago regarding the contemplative journey. Even though the book quoted many saints and mystics, the author never once mentioned Jesus. When this person asked me what I thought of the book, the only thing I could say was, "It is incomplete."

This mindset, I believe, reflects what is the greatest crisis in the world today: a lack of faith in the divinity of Christ. Very few people believe that Jesus is God. Interestingly, though, he remains very popular, since many consider him to be a philosopher, a holy person, or a prophet, and many other things. Basically, many people believe that Jesus is everything but God. Furthermore, if you asked me what the greatest crisis in the Church is, I would say it is a lack of Christians, including me, not rooting ourselves deeply enough in the divinity of Christ. In other words, it is Christians refusing to give up their own life so that Christ can live completely in them.

This may sound like a harsh criticism. Though I do not intend to be harsh, we must ask ourselves, what is the goal or point of the Christian life? It is very simple. It is to die. Jesus himself confirms this when he says, *"Unless a grain of wheat falls into the earth and dies, it remains alone; but if it dies, it bears much fruit"* (John 12:24). The death that Jesus calls us to is not primarily a physical death, though of course that will occur. Rather, it is a death to ourselves as the center of our lives.

Why must this death occur? So that Christ can live in and through us. In other words, so that our humanity can be transformed with his thoughts, words, sentiments, and actions, so that when people see us, listen to us, or speak to us, it is Christ they see, hear, and are speaking to. In essence, we can conclude that the purpose of the Christian life is to become another Christ. How do we do that? But allowing his presence to conquer us. St. Paul understood this perfectly when he wrote, *"For to me to live is Christ"* (Philippians 1:21) and *"It is no longer I who live, but Christ who lives in me"* (Galatians 2:20). What is St. Paul telling us? He is reminding us that we have no life; Christ is our life, completely and entirely.

In my experience of directing retreats, almost always when a priest or religious arrives they are burned out physically, emotionally, psychologically, or spiritually. Unfortunately, often it is not just in one of these areas, but in several, and even with some, all the above. Burnout, quite honestly, is a natural and even normal human experience, regardless of our vocation. However, a question I always ask them at the beginning of the retreat is: when was the last time you looked Jesus in the eye? In other words, what I am asking them is, when was the last time that prayer was an intimate exchange with him? And when was the last time you caught Jesus looking at you, loving you, and calling you? Maybe the last time you looked Jesus in the eye was an hour ago, but for many of us, it's been a while.

What happens when we are not looking Jesus in the eye? It's simple: life becomes an abstraction. In other words, we get stuck in our heads, and everything is a problem that I must solve or figure out. God becomes some mysterious and distant reality that I must try to get to or find. If we find ourselves stuck in our mind, endlessly thinking, worrying, or trying to make everything perfect, this is most likely a sign that we are not looking Jesus in the eye, or we are not, like Mary, "keeping all these things in our heart." St. Gregory of Nyssa reminds us of the importance of looking Jesus in the eye when he writes: *"We shall be blessed with clear vision if we keep our eyes fixed on Christ. . . . As no darkness can be seen by anyone surrounded by light, so no trivialities can capture the attention of anyone who has his eyes on Christ."*

CONCLUSION

As I have shown in this reflection, Mary is the model par excellence of the interior life. It is she who is always gazing deeply into the eyes of Jesus, and the One she sees in those eyes is not another guru, philosopher, or teacher, but God incarnate. She reminds us that we do not need secret methods of prayer, degrees in theology, or a stack of books to read to grow in the interior life. Of course, some of those things can be helpful, but Mary reminds us of the *"one thing needful"* (Luke 10:42), the presence of Jesus. Without his presence, our interior life, and really our entire life, will be incomplete.

Therefore, what is Mary's message to us? It is, and has always been, Jesus. If she were to write a book on the interior life, I am convinced that the title of the book would be simply *Jesus*. I could see the following as possible chapter titles written in the form of exhortations: Love Jesus, Follow Jesus, Trust Jesus, Desire Jesus, Surrender to Jesus, Pray to Jesus, All for Jesus. If we would ask her for some practical advice on how to do that she would say, "Remember." Remember the words, actions, and most especially, the presence of Jesus constantly in your heart. If we do this, she will assure us, as Jesus did, *"You will know the truth, and the truth will make you free"* (John 8:32).

11

Wedding Feast at Cana

The Presence of Mary

*"His mother said to the servants,
'Do whatever he tells you.'"*
—John 2:5

The presence of a mother

My mother was a rather simple and ordinary woman. She grew up in a small town, had a basic education, and almost never traveled. She was not interested in fashion or promoting herself in any way; in fact, she never expressed any interest in the things of this world. She was content with life as it was, and never sought to decorate her life with anything extra. After she married my father, she worked for a year in a sock factory until she became pregnant with my sister. Once she knew she was going to be a mother, she quit her job and remained at home for the next eighteen years, raising both my sister and me. My mother's whole world consisted of the simple, ordinary life of our family. That was enough for her.

One thing, though, that was extraordinary about my mother was her presence. Whether I was in trouble, whether I had done something good, whether I was happy or sad, regardless of my own experience or behavior, my mother's presence was always the same. It was always loving, accepting, and nurturing. In all the ups and downs of childhood, my mother's presence was the one constant and stable reality I could depend on. Several years ago, it occurred to me that without her motherhood, I could not be the man I am today. Hence, her loving, accepting, and nurturing presence strengthened me to become the man God was calling me to be.

Such is the power of motherhood. All of us, especially men, would be severely weakened without it. Its power, from my own experience, lies in its gentleness and in its ability to love and nurture life. Even though there is much conversation today regarding gender and gender roles, there is one thing I know: there is nothing on this planet like motherhood, and there is no substitute for it. Of course, I am speaking here about earthly motherhood, but this would apply to spiritual motherhood as well. Inside the heart and soul of every woman is a mother, whether she has physical children or not. At her very core, woman is mother, which is why genuine femininity is such a beautiful and necessary gift for our world.

MARY'S MOTHERLY PRESENCE AT CANA

In the wedding at Cana, Mary is revealed to us primarily as mother. In fact, throughout the Gospel of John, Mary is never called by her personal name, she is always referred to as the mother of Jesus. This occurs three times in the Gospel account of the wedding at Cana: *"The mother of Jesus was there"* (John 2:1), *"the mother of Jesus said to him"* (2:3), *"his mother said to the servants"* (2:5). The last place this occurs in St. John's Gospel is at the crucifixion: *"standing by the cross of Jesus were his mother . . ."* (John 19:25). In the mind and heart of St. John, Mary is first and foremost *mother*. She is, of course, the mother of Jesus, but also our mother who guides, forms, and nurtures our relationship with her Son.

What I find deeply moving about this Gospel is the initiative Mary takes in revealing to others who her Son is, but also in caring for the servers. These servers find themselves in a bit of a dilemma, having run out of wine at a wedding. This is not the end of the world, but it could become a source of embarrassment and humiliation for them, something that probably only a mother could foresee and be sensitive to. Mary approaches them and tells them to *"do whatever he tells you"* (John 2:5). Why do they listen to her? Most likely, they don't know who she is and they don't know who Jesus is, and on a surface level there is nothing deeply convincing or appealing about her words. Yet as soon as Jesus tells them to *"fill the jars with water"* (John 2:7), they respond without hesitation.

They listen to her, I believe, because they see and hear a mother who cares for them. They see and hear a mother who has sought them out, not for her own good but for theirs. Finally, they see and hear a mother who is motivated primarily by love: love for her Son and love for them. It is this tender and loving motherly presence that leads the servers to obey her words and to trust Jesus by doing whatever he tells them. And this in turn leads to Jesus's first public miracle and therefore the manifestation of his divinity.

MARY, THE MOTHER OF THE CONTEMPLATIVE LIFE

Someone recently asked me, "What is the most important lesson that you have learned while living as a hermit?" Without hesitation I responded, "Without Mary, our growth in the interior life will be limited." Recently, I was pleasantly surprised to discover that this was not an original thought of mine, but that others more learned and holier than I came to the same conclusion. For example, St. Gregory Palamas writes,

> Just as it was through her alone that He came to us, and "appeared on earth and lived among men" (Baruch 3:37), whereas previously He was invisible to all, so in the unending age that follows, any progress towards divine illumination, every revelation of the mysteries of the divine order, and every kind of spiritual gift is beyond the capacity of anyone, without her.[26]

Blessed Columba Marmion expresses this same reality in much simpler terms when he states: "When the mother is left out, the Son is no longer understood."[27] The point is clear; without Mary our interior life will be severely weakened. This is not merely my own opinion, but the testimony of many saints, theologians, and mystics through the ages.

Interestingly, many people suffer today from what is known as a "mother wound." Previously, "the father wound" was a more common occurrence. What these two wounds suggest is that a person had an unpleasant experience from one or both of their parents while growing up and this experience has caused a deep hurt within them. This hurt or wound affects their entire life, from being able to receive love from others, to trust issues, and even to how they relate to their own children. Everyone I have ever spoken with who suffers from one or both wounds describe a feeling deep inside that something has always been missing in their life. What is missing? The experience of safety, security, and unconditional love, that a parent has the responsibility, to the best of their ability, to provide to their children.

When I first became a priest, I heard about the "father wound" from many people in the sacrament of reconciliation and in spiritual direction. In the last several years, and the more I speak about Mary to people, the more I hear about this "mother wound." This mother wound, I have noticed, is perhaps the greatest obstacle that many people experience toward Mary. Many of these people have shared with me that they understand the biblical basis for devotion to Mary, they are aware of the testimony from the saints regarding the importance of Mary, and they understand and accept the Church's teachings on Mary. However, despite all of this, their hearts are still wounded, and they express to me how difficult it is to have a relationship with Mary because of their experience with their own mother. Just as the father wound can make us question the goodness and love of God the Father because of a negative experience of our earthly father, so too the mother wound can make us resistant and even fearful toward Mary because of a negative experience of our earthly mother.

When my own mother became ill with depression, I was filled with a variety of emotions that included sorrow, compassion, and anger. I was only eighteen years old at the time, and my heart experienced tremendous sorrow because not only was my mother sick, but also she was unable, at least physically and emotionally, to be the mother

I needed. Seeing her suffer led me to be compassionate, because I knew that not only was this illness causing me much pain, but also she was suffering tremendously. Strangely enough, though, I was also filled with anger at my mother. There was a part of me that felt, though I know this was not true, that my mother had given up on life and that if she really loved me and our family, she would get better. Hence, when I first started praying to Mary and developing my relationship with her, I was faced with the temptation to think, *Is she going to leave me also?* Thankfully, I never allowed myself to listen to that temptation that would prohibit me from developing my relationship with Mary.

If we are struggling with one or both wounds, we must be very patient and gentle with ourselves. We must acknowledge our struggle and not be ashamed by it, but with God's grace we must attempt as best we can to move through it. The primary reason for that is that God and Mary are nothing like even the best earthly fathers and mothers. Both are infinitely greater. Because Mary and of course God are infinitely greater, this is more reason for us to develop our relationship with them. Speaking specifically of Mary, St. John Bosco reminds us of this when he says, *"The fullness of love in all the mothers of this earth could never equal the love Mary has for each one of us."* Personally, in my time thus far living as a hermit, I am beginning to experience this truth more deeply, and is why I'm convinced that without her, our growth in the interior life will be limited.

FURTHER ILLUSTRATIONS

To illustrate this more deeply, let us consider a few more points. First, Mary shows us things we can't discover on our own. She showed the waiters at Cana that there was someone there who could help them. To those waiters Jesus was just another guest, and it was only through Mary that they discovered he was much more. Imagine if Mary was not present at the wedding. Would Jesus still have performed *"the first of his signs"* that *"manifested his glory" (John 2:11)*? Maybe he would have, but we will never know. However, what we do know is that Mary initiated this miracle by presenting the waiters' needs to Jesus and by exhorting them to *"do whatever he tells you" (John 2:5)*. Without Mary, not only would the waiters have been embarrassed and possibly humiliated, but even worse, they would never have had an encounter with Jesus. It was she who showed them the truth about her Son, a truth they would never have discovered on their own. Mary's love and concern for the waiters and the truth she showed them are exactly what Mary does in our lives if we allow her.

Second, Mary tells us things about Jesus that no book, theology course, or even saint can teach us. It is assumed that Mary is the one who provided St. Luke in his Gospel with all the details and events of Jesus's birth. Where else could he have acquired such intimate knowledge of the birth of Jesus if not from his mother? By the time St. Luke was writing his Gospel, St. Joseph had died, and therefore Mary was the only one who could provide St. Luke with the details and events of Jesus's early life. Without Mary, this intimate knowledge of her Son would be lost. Hence, there is no one who knows Jesus like Mary. Venerable Mary of Agreda in *The Mystical City of God* writes that *"from her first instant in the womb of her mother, she was wiser, more prudent, more enlightened, and more capable of comprehending God and all His works, than all the creatures have been or ever will be in eternity, excepting of course her only Son."*[28] This wisdom and enlightenment that Mary possesses, she desires to share with us, since she never keeps anything, especially her Son, simply for herself.

Finally, Mary protects the Incarnation. When we are close to Mary, we will always be close to the fruit of her womb, Jesus.

Therefore, when we are close to Mary, she will not allow us to drift off into some super-spiritual world that downplays the reality and importance of the Incarnation. Mary's presence always roots us in the real Jesus, who is the Son of God and the Son of Mary, the Word incarnate who was born of her, suffered, died, and is risen from the dead. In Mary Jesus is not another prophet, he is not another religious leader, and he is not another holy man. Rather, he is the Messiah and Savior of all humanity. He is the One whom we must know, love, and serve. Hence, when we understand and are close to Mary, we understand and are closer to Jesus. Or, as the *Catechism of the Catholic Church* states: "*What the Catholic faith believes about Mary is based on what it believes about Christ, and what it teaches about Mary illumines in turn its faith in Christ*" (CCC 487).

In essence, Mariology is the best safeguard for Christology. In other words, by understanding who Mary is, we understand more deeply who Jesus is. For example, Jesus is God. Mary gives birth to Jesus. Therefore, Mary is the Mother of God. By proclaiming Mary as Mother of God, we are proclaiming that Jesus is Lord. Second, Jesus as God is all pure and all holy. For God to take flesh and enter our world, not only would it be appropriate and just, but also necessary, that he would enter our world through an all-holy and all-pure vessel. Hence, Mary is immaculately conceived. Her immaculate conception proclaims Christ's divinity. Finally, St. Paul reminds us that "*Christ being raised from the dead will never die again; death no longer has dominion over him*" (Romans 6:9). In Jesus's resurrection we glimpse our future destiny. Is it too hard to believe that God would bring that destiny already to its completion in his Mother in her Assumption? Mary's Assumption then affirms and proclaims the truth of Easter, that Christ is risen, and Resurrection is our destiny.

If we are close to Mary, then, we never have to worry about being far away from God, because wherever God is, Mary is. For all these reasons then and many more, Mary has an insight, experience, and knowledge that are all together special and unique and that we desperately need.

THE PRESENCE OF MARY—A COMFORT AND CONSOLATION

Throughout my life as a Franciscan, many people have shared with me their stories of returning to the faith. I have also heard many stories from priests and nuns who have suffered serious doubts and trials regarding their vocation. Some of them were seriously considering leaving the priesthood or religious life. Throughout all these stories, I have heard the full spectrum of our human drama, a spectrum that includes sin, tragedy, and heartache. Yet in all these different stories I have listened with amazement and wonder at the mystery of God's grace in each one of their lives. In almost every story, I have noticed a recurring theme. The theme is Mary. Each person, in their own way, made a more intentional decision to turn to her amid their struggles. Even though they may already have had a relationship with her, their current crisis inspired them to turn even more deeply to her than they had before in their life.

If somebody were to ask me what happened to each one of these people, I would simply say, "Mary is what happened to them." Amid their confusion, pain, and brokenness, by turning more deeply to her, they found in her that loving, accepting, and nurturing mother whose presence, in a very real way, dried their tears. Once those tears were dry, Mary did what she has always done: she took them by the hand and led them back to the presence of her Son. It is then no surprise that each of these people have been able to find their way through darkness back to Jesus, *"the light of the world" (John 8:12)*.

St. Aelred writes that *"Through her (Mary) we have been born, not for the world, but for God."* The light and beauty of Mary's presence breaks through our human drama, and she shows us not *what* we are made for, but *who* we are made for. Mary's presence reminds us that we are created only for Jesus and that to live for him, in him, and through him, we must heed the words of St. Paul to *"seek the things that are above, where Christ is,"* and to set our *"minds on things that are above, not on the things of earth. For you have died, and your life is hidden with Christ in God" (Colossians 3:1–3).* Hence, once we become aware of the presence of Mary in our lives, we will never be the same. Lest anyone think this may be merely a pious hope, all we must do is turn to the Gospels for validation.

It is the presence of Mary that reminds St. Joseph of God's will (Matthew 1:20–21). After the star of Bethlehem, it is the presence of Mary that reveals to the Magi where they will find the newborn king (Matthew 2:11). It is the presence of Mary that strengthens Elizabeth at the Visitation (Luke 1:41–42). It is the presence of Mary that consoles the apostles after the Crucifixion (Acts 1:14). And, strangely enough, it is the presence of Mary that will console Jesus during his entire earthly life, from her holding him in her arms as a baby, to her initiating his first miracle at the wedding in Cana, and to her remaining faithfully by his side during the Passion. Mary's presence is always a comfort and a consolation, even to God himself.

What is true in this regard for God, is true for us. Through Mary, God shares with us his own comfort and consolation. Hence, Mary's consoling motherly presence is God's will for us, and because it is God's will for us, it is something Mary desires also. Let us then not refuse either the will of God or the desire of Mary, and let us receive more deeply the gift of her motherly presence in each of our lives.

12

Behold, Your Mother

Finding God amid Suffering

"He said to the disciple, 'Behold, your mother.' And from that hour the disciple took her to his own home."
—John 19:27

GOD IS RIGHT HERE

Several years ago, a preacher told a story that I will never forget. The story, the preacher told us, came from a Jewish man whose grandmother spent two years living in Auschwitz. According to his grandmother, one day in the concentration camp a 12-year-old boy was caught stealing bread from the Nazis. He was stealing bread, she said, in the hopes of helping a fellow prisoner who was greatly malnourished. The Nazis immediately took the boy and called the entire camp to gather in the main square. When everyone had gathered, the Nazi commander stood in the middle of the square with the boy and explained to everyone what had occurred. After the commander finished recounting the story, he said in a stern voice to the whole camp, "nobody steals from the Nazis."

The commander then tied a rope to a branch from a tree and tied the other end around the boy's neck and addressed the camp once again, "this is what happens if you steal from the Nazis." There, in front of everyone, he hanged him. The entire camp was in shock. A few seconds later, after they began to process what had just occurred, several loud gasps echoed throughout the camp, while many others wailed aloud furiously. After a minute or so a prisoner cried out, "Where is God?" A few seconds later, another prisoner responded, "God is right here."

Suffering, even for the holiest person, has a traumatic effect on us. It forces us to pause for a moment, not in order to entertain doubt, but in order to choose once again to believe despite the confusion and anguish one experiences amid suffering. Wondering or even questioning where God is amid suffering is a universal experience, even for the person with faith. St. Martha herself says to Jesus after the death of her brother, Lazarus, *"Lord, if you had been here, my brother would not have died"* (John 11:21).

Most of us have never lived in a concentration camp, yet all of us have experienced death, suffering, heartache, and so many other things that have forced us to cry out at times, "Where is God?" Where is God amidst my own personal suffering, whether it be physical, emotional, or psychological? Where is God amidst the immense suffering of the world, whether it be from war, disease, or sin? Where is God in the seemingly endless scandals in the Church, in politics, and in human relationships in general? These are honest questions that all of us must ask. Asking them does not imply a lack of faith, but rather reflects a genuine desire within the human heart to know the truth.

In St. John's account of the crucifixion, the very last act of Jesus before he dies is to give his mother to John: *"Behold, your mother!" (John 19:27)*. Why is Mary given to St. John and us at the cross? There are many reasons, some of which we have already reflected on in this book. However, I believe the primary reason is because each one of us is like that voice that cries out, "Where is God?" Where is God in my suffering, in my confusion, and heartache? It is Mary who reminds us, "He is right here." She is that lone voice that can assure us that suffering does not disprove God's existence, but in fact it becomes an invitation to a greater intimacy and depth with God if we can allow ourselves to go through it.

WITHOUT MARY CHRISTIANITY/DISCIPLESHIP IS INCOMPLETE

Many of us have had the experience of being with someone when they died. Death is an extraordinary experience filled with reverence and mystery. There is no moment in life like death and because of this the last words and actions of a dying person are extremely significant. A person's last words or actions reveal in many ways the heart of the person dying and often provide a memory for their loved ones to hold on to and cherish for the rest of their life.

My mother spent the last 15 years of her life in a nursing home suffering from depression and Alzheimer's. Over the years her mind and her speech became less coherent, and she became outwardly a different person from the mother I knew growing up. When she was transferred to hospice care I knew that her time was limited. I, along with my father and sister, prayed at her side, and I anointed her and gave her last rites. Afterward we all said "I love you" to her and she, as best as she could, responded by saying "I love you." Shortly after, she slipped into a coma and died a day later. Those were the last words I would ever hear her say. Hearing my mother utter those words, despite the suffering and mental decline she had experienced, I was reminded of the mother I knew as a boy. And, at least to my ears, she sounded like that same mother as well. It is a memory that I am both grateful to God for and one that I will always cherish for the rest of my life.

The last action that Jesus performs before he dies is to entrust Mary to St. John: *"Behold, your mother!"* (John 19:27). We are told then that *"from that hour the disciple took her to his own home"* (John 19:27). This verse alone contains an enormous wealth of theological reflection and spiritual insight. However, as rich as this verse is, the next verse is just as profound. St. John tells us, *"After this Jesus, knowing that all was now finished, said . . ., 'I thirst'"* (John 19:28). After Jesus gives Mary to John, we are told that "all was now finished." The gift of Mary to St. John is the final action of the Savior of the world. The entrustment of the disciple to Mary and of Mary to the disciple, then, is a significant part of the plan of redemption, since it is only after this action that *"all is now finished."*

The "beloved disciple" in St. John's Gospel is St. John himself. However, he represents all the disciples of the Lord throughout history, and therefore each of us can include ourselves as the beloved disciple also. Hence, whatever Jesus says and does to the beloved disciple in St. John's Gospel, he is intending for us as well. Therefore, just as Mary is given to St. John at the Crucifixion, she is also given to you and me. St. John Paul II affirms this when he writes, *"The Mother of Christ, who stands at the very center of this mystery . . . is given as mother to every single individual and all mankind."*

There are many implications stemming from this. However, the one I find most profound is this: following Jesus with Mary at our side is what Christian discipleship is meant to look like. It is inconceivable, then, in God's mind, to imagine or attempt to follow Jesus without Mary. We cannot truly be disciples of Jesus without her. Therefore, it is impossible to have a deep life of prayer, an "effective" ministry, and to love as Jesus calls us to love, without her. Just as Mary was the will of the Father for Jesus, so too is Mary the will of the Father and Jesus for us. St. Louis de Montfort states this in very bold terms when he writes,

> *Just as in natural and bodily generation there is a father and a mother, so in the supernatural and spiritual generation there is a father who is God and a mother who is Mary. All true children of God have God for their father and Mary for their mother; anyone who does not have Mary for his mother does not have God for his father.*[29]

In my life as a priest, whenever I am meeting with someone who is struggling, whether in marriage, ministry, or in prayer, my first question to them is always, "Where is Mary?" Specifically, I am asking them, "Are you consciously living your life with her?" Often the answer to that question is no, not because these people don't love her or don't have a relationship with her, but simply because they have forgotten about her importance in the life of discipleship. If the fullness of discipleship consists in following Jesus with Mary, as Jesus reveals to us at the Cross, then Mary cannot be someone we turn to only occasionally for help and guidance. Her role in our life is meant to be an active one, since we are meant to live our entire lives as Christians with her. Therefore, we must strive to be consciously with her, spiritually, mentally, and even physically.

In my own life, I have realized that when I am not intentionally following Jesus with Mary, discipleship is more difficult. Things like prayer, ministry, and fraternal love, none of which are ever easy, feel even more challenging. It has become very clear to me then that without her, my vocation and all that it entails is incomplete. This is not meant to imply that if we have Mary in our life we will never suffer. Neither Jesus nor Mary was spared suffering, and despite what some may think, we will not be spared suffering either. However, Mary's presence, I have noticed, both softens and strengthens our hearts and minds toward suffering because she is that lone voice telling us and reminding us, "God is right here." St. Maximilian Kolbe expresses this in a most beautiful image when he writes,

> *In Mary's womb our soul must be reborn after the form of Jesus Christ. She is bound to feed the soul with the milk of her grace, raise it as lovingly as she nourished, looked after, and raised Jesus. At her knee the soul must learn to know and love Jesus.*[30]

SUFFERING WITH GOD

It is then from the Cross that Jesus reveals to us the importance of Mary in our life of discipleship. However, from the Cross Mary reveals to us another important aspect of discipleship. This truth is a difficult one, and one many of us, including me, would rather meditate on instead of participate in. One will find very few sermons preached on this subject, and there are very few books written on it. It is the truth that if we desire to become mature disciples, we must be willing to suffer for God and with God. What could this possibly mean?

It is not uncommon for beginners in the spiritual life to seek out and desire consolations and to acquire experiences of God. I did this for many years in the beginning of my spiritual life, and I have listened to many young men and women, both in religious life and those in the world, who have done the same. Without realizing it, and without consciously willing it, beginners in the spiritual life often use God in an attempt to make themselves feel good. They associate with God himself the consolations and experiences that occur in prayer, spiritual conversation, or certain ascetic disciplines. And because these experiences feel good on a natural and sensory level, for the beginner they become synonymous with the presence of God. After all, these feelings occur in the middle of or after spiritual exercises. Therefore, if I don't feel something, the beginner often thinks, something must be wrong with my spiritual life, since I have equated consolations and experiences as the evidence of God's presence.

St. John of the Cross, a tremendous spiritual director of extraordinary insight, describes this way what is really happening in the life of beginners in the spiritual life:

> *They find its joy in spending lengthy periods of prayer, its penances are pleasures, its fasts happiness, and the sacraments and spiritual conversations are its consolations. Although they practice these exercises with great profit and persistence . . . they conduct themselves in a very weak and imperfect manner. Their motivation in their spiritual works and exercises is the consolation and satisfaction they experience in them.*[31]

This is a very challenging assessment. One can easily be discouraged while reading St. John of the Cross's words about the motivation of a beginner. However, it's important to keep in mind that consolations and experiences of God are necessary for our spiritual life. If God grants them, we should never dismiss them. God uses consolations, and he gives us tangible, sensible experiences of him at times to strengthen us. The problem becomes when we seek the consolations and experiences rather than the living God, or when we seek the consolations of God and not God himself. We then pray and live the spiritual life in general because of how it makes us feel.

What St. John of the Cross is describing is the motivation that often accompanies the beginner in the spiritual life. Mary at the cross shows us what mature discipleship looks like. What then does that look like? It is being willing to suffer for God and with God, as she did. When this transformation occurs within us, we have now begun to walk on more solid ground, leaving behind the way of the beginner and embarking on a deeper path that leads to genuine holiness.

To illustrate this more deeply I would like to share a quote from St. Bonaventure. He says that when Mary

> saw the love of the Eternal Father towards men to be so great that, in order to save them, He willed the death of His Son, and, on the other hand, seeing the love of the Son in wishing to die for us: in order to conform herself to this excessive love of both the Father and the Son towards the human race, she also with her entire will offered, and consented to, the death of her Son, in order that we might be saved.[32]

St. Bonaventure is saying that Mary sees the love of the Father in giving us his Son. She sees the love of the Son in dying for us. Because her love toward both the Father and Son is so great, she wishes to imitate this tremendous love. In a sense, she asks herself, "How can I imitate the love of the Father and the Son?" She answers that question by offering her will to God and by consenting to the death of her Son. In short, she consents to the death of her Son, and by doing so, she allows herself to suffer for God and with God.

Mary could have run away from Good Friday; after all, most of Jesus's disciples did. Mary could have said, "No, this isn't fair, this isn't right, this is not the way it should be." However, Mary didn't run away from Calvary. Despite the suffering it entailed, she never left Jesus. In a mysterious way, she allowed herself to be crucified with him on Good Friday, and by doing so she revealed to us what love for God really looks like.

Mary sees and lives the Crucifixion, and suffering in general, much differently than we do. Mary views suffering as an opportunity for self-gift. Mary sees suffering as an opportunity to love God. And how does she do that? Amid suffering, especially at the death of her Son, she surrenders her will entirely to God and accepts with profound trust whatever God allows. In other words, suffering for God and with God is, as Mary shows us at the cross, the path of mature discipleship. Holiness ultimately is not about consolations and experiences, as important as they are, but holiness consists in our willingness to suffer for God and with God when it is asked of us. This takes tremendous courage, faith, and love, all of which Mary possesses in abundance.

PRACTICAL APPLICATION

Mary's Motherhood at the cross is a mysterious mixture of both gentleness and strength. It is gentle because if, like St. John, we bring her more deeply into our lives, we will experience her tenderness and delicacy toward both our spiritual and physical needs. In fact, Mary is so gentle that most of the time we don't even perceive her care and presence in our life. However, were she not there, our life, especially our relationship with God, would look much different. Hence, we do not need to look for Mary in our lives, but rather to realize that she is already there. One Marian soul expressed it this way: *"It was necessary, not to put the Blessed Virgin in my spiritual life, but to find her there, to realize her maternal role."*[33]

Even though Mary was given by Jesus to John for him to take care of her, what really occurred was the opposite; she was taking care of him. Her care was not limited to St. John but was extended to all the disciples. It was she who was forming them and strengthening them by her motherly presence. Jesus willed it to be this way for the disciples, and it is what he wills for us.

Mary's motherhood at the cross is also an experience of strength. True strength can be found, not in our muscles, but in our willingness to suffer in faith, as Mary does at the cross. No matter what the trials, tragedies, and sufferings that we have faced or will face in this life, Mary has been there. Regardless of how much I have suffered in my life, I know for certain that Mary has suffered more. She knows, not theoretically, but with her whole being, what suffering is and how it feels. Therefore, in my own suffering I can find in Mary the strength necessary to carry the crosses that Jesus has given me.

What specifically is this strength that Mary gives me? It is a necessary reminder that I do not have to be afraid of suffering. Why? Because God is there. Therefore, whatever difficulties and hardships I may have to face in the future I can rest assured that I am not alone, because God is mysteriously present. Also, in my own growth in holiness I can choose, when God allows it, to suffer both with God and for God, and therefore use everything that happens in this life as a means to greater depth and intimacy with God. We cannot do this without Mary. We need both her gentleness and her strength. Of course, Jesus knew that, and this is why he gave her to us at the Cross.

13

Mary and the Apostles at Prayer

The Contemplative Rosary

"All these with one accord devoted themselves to prayer, together with the women and Mary the mother of Jesus."
—Acts 1:14

Running into Ourselves

Prayer has been a major part of my life for the past 25 years. During that time, I have spoken with many people about prayer, and I have listened to many people share with me their thoughts on prayer and what prayer looks like in their personal lives. This conversation has been a major source of grace and blessings for me personally, primarily because it always inspires me to want to become a man of prayer. Amid all this conversation, I have determined that the first rule of prayer, or at least what our main priority in prayer must be, is to simply stop looking at ourselves. All of us, including me, to varying degrees, are self-obsessed.

I am often the first person I think of when I wake up, and the last person I think of when I go to bed. Unfortunately, this self-obsession does not merely occur at the beginning and end of our day. Most of us throughout the day exert a great deal of energy and spend a lot of time thinking about ourselves. We think about how other people perceive us, how we are going to spend our free time, and what we really need in our life at this moment to be happy. If we are honest, most of our daydreams have us at the center as well. We daydream about a life where everything goes the way we desire, where we have time to do everything we want, and where people appreciate and love us unconditionally. Though self-reflection is important, both for psychological and spiritual growth, our reflections about ourselves can often become obsessions with ourselves. Hence the urgent need, especially in a life of prayer, to stop thinking about ourselves, even if only for a few minutes.

Many years ago, I was the postulant director for my religious community. Postulancy is the first stage of formation in religious life. The young men who entered this stage had just recently left behind them a career, family, and friends and moved to New York City to discern more deeply if God was calling them to be a Franciscan. All these men were very passionate, idealistic, and energetic, but also very young. As the postulant director, I was the one responsible for them, and I was the one they looked to for advice about everything, ranging from prayer to fraternal living to working with the poor.

During their nine months as postulants, I would meet individually with each one of them every other week to see how they were doing. As the weeks and months progressed, I noticed that most of their struggles occurred, whether in ministry, prayer, or fraternal living, because they kept running into themselves. They would be frustrated with prayer if they were not being consoled, or if it wasn't going the way they thought it should. If the poor we were serving were not interested in them, they would often pull back and show little interest in the poor. If another brother thought differently or didn't see them the way they viewed themselves or the way their friends and family viewed them before they entered religious life, then they were quick to dismiss the other brother and conclude that something was wrong with him.

When I would mention this to them in our meetings, they would often get frustrated with themselves and resolve to try hard to forget themselves. Yet this, ironically, became another form of self-obsession. I would remind them gently, but also firmly, that there is more here than just you. In other words, prayer, ministry, fraternal life, and discipleship in general are not primarily about you. It is not about your own success, being recognized or doing everything perfectly. If you are recognized, appreciated, or even do everything perfectly, that is great, but there is something more important in discipleship than all of this.

I would assure them that the way they were acting was quite normal. In other words, running into themselves repeatedly was not a new phenomenon that began with them. Since discipleship is not an achievement we acquire based upon our own strength and ability, the more we begin to turn away from ourselves and turn more completely to God, the less interested we become in ourselves. Prayer then is a great liberation from ourselves, a vacation from our self-obsession. How then can we stop running into ourselves? Since there are many ways of prayer, there are many ways that can help us from repeating this normal human pattern. For me, the best way I have discovered is the Rosary, and the best person to help facilitate this self-transcendence is, of course, Mary.

In the Acts of the Apostles, shortly before Pentecost, we are told that the Apostles were gathered in the upper room with Mary in prayer. *"All these with one accord devoted themselves to prayer, together with . . . Mary, the mother of Jesus" (Acts 1:14).* This, I believe, is the perfect image of what the prayer of the Rosary is meant to be like. Through the Rosary, we are gathered with Mary as she turns us away from ourselves and toward her Son.

A CONTEMPLATIVE ROSARY

Without intending to sound overly dramatic, I can say unequivocally that the Rosary has saved my life, and it continues to do so each day. When my mother first became sick with depression and Alzheimer's, I was eighteen years old. I was not, at that time, praying regularly or attending Mass weekly. I was, like many teenagers, completely self-absorbed. My mother's illness left me deeply confused, alone, and in pain. I desperately needed a mother to turn to, and since my mother was sick and suffering psychologically, she was not available.

Thankfully, my father had a great devotion to Mary and the Rosary. All throughout our house there were rosaries and images of Mary in almost every room. One day I took one of those rosaries, went into my room, and began to pray. The way I prayed the Rosary, I would discover later, was very different from most people. I prayed it like a contemplative. I would pray a decade and sit in silence for two minutes, five minutes, and maybe even longer. Then, I would pray another decade and return to silence. It would take me about an hour to pray a whole Rosary (five decades), because the combination of the prayers, the mysteries of each decade, and the gradual turning away from my own self-absorption and toward God left a profound peace in my soul that prohibited me from praying the Rosary at a rapid pace. It wasn't until I began attending daily Mass at my parish, where they prayed the Rosary before Mass each morning, that I realized my way of praying the Rosary was not common.

I noticed very quickly that through the Rosary my whole being—body, mind, and soul—was turning more deeply toward God. I began to turn less toward myself. Of course, I would get distracted at times, restless, and even bored, but overall, when I was praying the Rosary, I was more focused on God than on myself. This was, and continues to be today, a tremendous gift and blessing. Hence, praying the Rosary caused a deeper stillness, silence, and peace within me. It is no surprise then why I took my time praying the Rosary and why I never wanted to stop.

At first, I began to ask myself, why are this stillness, silence, and peace occurring within me through the Rosary? Many people attribute a certain calmness and stillness to the repetition of the prayers of the Rosary or simply holding the rosary in one's hand. Though this is true to a certain extent, the deeper reason for the power of the Rosary is because through it we begin to wake up to the beauty, love, and truth of Jesus Christ. Every day when I went into my room to pray the Rosary, I was beginning to wake up more and more, not only to the truth of Jesus Christ, but also to the reality of his presence in me. Through the Rosary, especially when we pray it in this contemplative way, Jesus becomes more and more familiar to us, not just in our heads but in our hearts. The more familiar Jesus becomes to us, the greater our experience becomes of his love and mercy. When this occurs, our fears and anxieties begin to diminish, at least a little, and this allows us to open our hearts and minds more deeply to him.

It should be no surprise then that the Rosary is my favorite prayer. I always promote it and recommend it to people as much as I can—however, with this one distinction: I never encourage people to pray the Rosary. Rather, I always encourage them to pray a "contemplative Rosary." What is a contemplative Rosary? It is a Rosary that is prayed quietly, slowly, and without haste. I always tell people, "If you only have twenty minutes to pray the Rosary, please don't rush it. It is better to say two or three decades well, with silence in between each decade, than to simply rush through a whole Rosary devoid of interior prayer and recollection."

For some reason I have noticed, we tend to have this notion that the Rosary is something we must get through, perhaps to check off on our spiritual to-do list, rather than a great mystery we are being invited to enter. I often hear people say, "I have to get my Rosary in," a phrase that causes me a great deal of sadness, because it implies an obligatory and rigid approach to the Rosary. "Getting our Rosary in" may help us to build the habit of praying the Rosary, but I'm not sure it will enable us to experience its deeply contemplative nature. Msgr. Romano Guardini echoes this sentiment when he writes, "*The rosary is a prayer of lingering. One must take one's time for it, not only externally, but internally. . . . It is not necessary to ramble through the whole rosary. It is better to say only one or two decades, and to say them right.*"[34]

What I learned rather quickly through the Rosary, and what Romano Guardini seems to be saying, is that the Rosary is meant to be a time of silence, a time of listening and gazing with Mary at her Son. What is most important in the Rosary is the quality of love and attention that we give to that listening and to that gazing with Mary at Jesus.

Over the years, many people have shared with me their struggles with the Rosary. I began to struggle as well with the Rosary when

I entered religious life, and we prayed the Rosary each night in community. Since I wasn't used to praying it so fast, or at least at the pace it is often prayed when in a group, it began to lose its contemplative quality for me. I began to experience the Rosary as a burden and simply did my best merely to get through it. After I made my first vows with the Franciscans, the communal Rosary was now optional, so after night prayer I would retire to my room, light a candle in front of an icon of Mary, and pray the Rosary in my normal contemplative fashion. Once I did this, I began to experience once again its depth and beauty.

When I have spoken to people who are struggling with the Rosary and I recommend that they try praying a contemplative Rosary, their experience, for the most part, begins to change. This should not surprise us. Pope Paul VI says that *"Without contemplation the rosary is a body without a soul."* In other words, without this contemplative dimension the Rosary is incomplete, and perhaps one of the main reasons we struggle with the Rosary is because we forget it is primarily a form of contemplative prayer. Contemplative prayer is more concerned with resting in God and deeply savoring his presence, rather than discursively meditating or imagining different aspects of God. Hence, in contemplative prayer we are not so much thinking about him or imagining him, but simply being with him in simplicity, purity, and in silence, something the Rosary naturally leads us to if we give it the space and time that it deserves.

In my own life, I often pray all 20 mysteries of the Rosary each day. However, that is not my goal, nor is it something I feel I must do. Rather, I allow the Rosary to lead me throughout the day, in times of silent prayer, when I'm walking, before bed, and in any other moments throughout the day. In an hour of prayer I might say five decades, while I am on a walk I might say two or three, in Eucharistic adoration I might say another five decades, and in other moments throughout the day I may say a few more decades. Praying the Rosary this way, at least for me, enables me to spend most of my day gazing lovingly upon Jesus with Mary. Since I am never in a rush when I am praying the Rosary and since I have no agenda regarding how many decades I should say, the Rosary creates a contemplative space within me that carries over into every aspect of my life.

THE ROSARY: A CHRISTOCENTRIC PRAYER

Throughout this book we have witnessed a basic truth about Mariology: that everything we teach and believe about Mary enhances our faith, our understanding, and our love for Jesus. Hence, sometimes in theology we make the claim that it is Mariology, understanding who Mary is, that best promotes and defends Christology, understanding who Jesus is. *The Catechism of the Catholic Church* states it thus: *"What the Catholic faith believes about Mary is based on what it believes about Christ, and what it teaches about Mary illumines in turn its faith in Christ"* (CCC 487). Therefore, we can make the following conclusion: everything Marian is Christocentric because Mary's entire being is Christ-centered. This is also true regarding the Rosary. The Rosary is first and foremost a Christocentric prayer because it has Christ at the center. What then is Mary's role in the Rosary? It is one of mother and teacher.

St. John Paul II, reflecting on Mary's role in the Rosary, writes,

> She (Mary) kept all these things, pondering them in her heart" (Luke 2:19, cf 2:51). The memories of Jesus, impressed upon her heart, were always with her, leading her to reflect on the various moments of her life at her Son's side. In a way those memories were to be the "rosary," which she recited uninterruptedly throughout her earthly life. In the recitation of the rosary, the Christian community enters into contact with the memories and the contemplative gaze of Mary.[35]

In the Rosary, as in life, Mary is our mother and teacher. It is her "memories" of Jesus, as St. John Paul II beautifully exclaims, that become the heart of the Rosary. Through those memories Mary takes us by the hand, revealing to us the beauty and truth of her Son. If we really want to know Jesus, we can have no better teacher than Mary. In a similar way, if I want to learn how to speak Spanish well, I must find someone who is fluent in Spanish, who knows the language inside and out, with all its nuances, its slang, and its grammar. Hence, if I want to learn about Jesus, then I must go to Mary, whose very heart is filled with these "memories," these memories that I come into deeper contact with every time I pray the Rosary. As we can see then, in the Rosary we are contemplating the mystery of Christ with Mary. What occurs next is truly miraculous. We begin to stop running into ourselves, and we finally begin to start running into Jesus!

Sr. Lucia, one of the visionaries at Fatima, once said that *"There is no problem, no matter how difficult it is, whether temporal or above all spiritual, in the personal life of each one of us, of our families . . . that cannot be solved by the rosary."* What Sr. Lucia is reminding us of is that there is nothing the Rosary can't handle. How can she make such a bold claim? It's very simple. The Rosary is nothing else but the Gospel of Jesus Christ, and Jesus is ultimately the answer to all our problems. When we immerse ourselves in him, into these "memories" of Mary, we cannot help being transformed.

Outside of the liturgy and the sacraments, there has been no prayer greater than the Rosary in all of Christendom. Since it was first given to us in the thirteenth century, it has converted millions of people and deepened the faith of countless souls. Through the Rosary people have found healing, faith, and hope. Some, by praying the Rosary regularly, have discovered their vocations, while others, through the Rosary, have been given the grace to forgive. Everyone who prays the Rosary encounters a deepening in their interior life, because through the Rosary they are encountering Jesus Christ. And yet the Rosary does not belong merely to a specific ethnic group, social class, or education level. Rather, the Rosary is for the rich and the poor, the young and the old, the saints and the sinners.

Because of its contemplative and Christocentric nature, the Rosary is a powerful, and I would argue, necessary component for our Christian life. It has become somewhat vogue in our culture to see people wearing the rosary as jewelry or to see it hanging in cars or windows. I was walking one time in Lower Manhattan when a man approached me and asked me if I had a rosary. I reached into my pocket, gave him my rosary, and asked him if he knew how to pray it. "Oh," the man said, "I'm not going to pray it. I just heard that if you have one it will bring you good luck." I immediately took the rosary back and said to him "the rosary will bring you something more than good luck, it will bring you Jesus, but only if you pray it." He looked at me somewhat surprised and humbly asked me, "Will you teach me to pray it?" "There is nothing else I would rather do," I said to him. There amid thousands of people walking past us on the busy streets of New York City, I shared with him the power and beauty of the Rosary. I am confident that if he is still praying the Rosary today, his life is very different now, because he has been transformed by these memories of Mary.

14

The Woman Clothed with the Sun

The Assumption: Glimpsing Our Destiny

"A great sign appeared in heaven, a woman clothed with the sun, with the moon under her feet, and on her head a crown of twelve stars."
—Revelation 12:1

Holiness takes us beyond ourselves

All of us who are disciples of Christ and who are striving to follow him each day are walking on the path of holiness. The sacraments, prayer, and the love of neighbor are all means of grace for us on this journey that help us to *"love the Lord your God with all your heart, and with all your soul, and with all your strength, and with all your mind; and your neighbor as yourself" (Luke 10:27).* This path of holiness is filled with twists and turns that take us through deserts, valleys, and mountains. This path includes moments of consolation and desolation, times of both overwhelming brightness and abysmal dark nights, and most of all it includes the daily fluctuation between clarity and confusion and between love and selfishness.

Even though many of us are on this journey, few of us reach the end of it in this life. Though it is true that the path of holiness does not end in this life, the Church shows us what holiness looks like in her different saints. Those characteristics include things like heroic virtue and a life conformed totally to the gospel, and often will include miraculous or supernatural happenings in the life of the saint. Even though there are many saints, there are many more people who have not become saints. Consequently, holiness in this life is rare. To prove this point, all we must do is realize that very few of us become canonized saints. Though it is true that not every holy person becomes a canonized saint, the truth remains that most of us will end our lives still on this journey of holiness.

If holiness in this life is rare, then encountering a holy person in this life is also rare. If we were to be blessed by such an encounter, it would appear obvious that this could have the potential of being a life-changing event, something we would never forget. Many of the older Franciscans in my community met and even knew St. Teresa of Calcutta. A few not only knew St. Teresa but were also friends with her. When she would come to New York she would call them and arrange for them to speak and teach her sisters. Because of their close affiliation with St. Teresa, many other friars were able to meet her and speak with her, even if only for a few seconds.

When I was a postulant and then a novice, it was not uncommon to hear some of these friars recount either meeting St. Teresa or reminisce about the time they spent with her. Every time I would listen to them, their response was always the same: they were like children filled with excitement, awe, and wonder. It was beautiful to witness. These same friars could have been previously telling jokes or goofing around, and as soon as St. Teresa's name was mentioned their whole demeanor changed because of the reverence and love they had for her.

Such is the effect that holiness can have on us. The power of the saints is that they take us out of ourselves and beyond ourselves. Thankfully, we do not necessarily have to meet saints in person to be affected by their holiness. This can occur simply by reading about them, which is why it is necessary that we become familiar with the saints and develop a relationship with them. St. Ignatius of Loyola's whole conversion occurred while reading about the lives of the saints. After being struck in the leg with a cannon ball during the Battle of Pamplona in 1521, St. Ignatius was confined to bed, where he had nothing else to do but read. Interestingly, the only books that were available to him were religious ones, specifically books about the lives of the saints. Having been a worldly man until this point, he found that reading now about the lives of the saints inspired him so deeply that when he recovered from his injuries he became a soldier of Christ. The saints, through their lives of holiness, took him out of himself and beyond himself.

If this is true regarding the holiness of the saints, how much more is this true with Mary? St. Maximilian Kolbe writes that *"the single desire of the Immaculata [Mary] is to raise the level of our spiritual life to the summits of holiness.*"[36] As we have seen throughout this book, every time we encounter Mary in the Scriptures, in the Liturgy, and in our personal life, she always takes us out of ourselves and beyond ourselves. In this last chapter, Mary will continue to do just that. However, this time she will take us even further, into eternity itself.

THE ASSUMPTION

The first reading for the Solemnity of the Assumption of Mary on August 15 is taken from the book of Revelation 12:1–6. The reading begins, *"A great sign appeared in heaven, a woman clothed with the sun, with the moon under her feet, and on her head a crown of twelve stars" (Revelation 12:1).* Throughout Christian history the common interpretation of this passage is that the mysterious woman in Revelation 12 is Mary. The Church, by using this reading in the liturgy for the Assumption, not only confirms this teaching but also uses it to direct our hearts and minds to the transcendent beauty of Mary's Assumption and what it means for us.

What then exactly are we celebrating in this feast? There are, I believe, two main things. First, we are celebrating Mary's Passover from this world directly into heaven, where she is right now immersed in the fullness of the beatific vision, in all its brightness and glory. Mary, the dogma of the Assumption teaches, is living fully the resurrected life, since her body and soul dwell together now in heaven. In other words, Mary is already complete. This is not true for us. When we die our body and soul will not be united until after the general judgment.

For Mary, there is no waiting necessary. She is already living in that fullness and glory of God that will one day, God willing, be ours as well. This should not surprise us at all. St. Bernadine of Siena writes: *"The likeness between God's Mother and her divine Son, in the way of the nobility and dignity of body and soul—a likeness that forbids us to think of the heavenly Queen as being separated from the heavenly king."*[37]

Part of the basis for the teaching of the dogma of the Assumption can be found as a logical outcome of another Marian dogma: the Immaculate Conception. Because sin is ultimately the cause of death, and because Mary is sinless, she escapes the corruption (separation of body and soul, and decay of the body), that occurs after death and therefore enters immediately into glory.

The Assumption can be found as a logical outcome of another Marian dogma: the Immaculate Conception. Because sin is ultimately the cause of death, and because Mary is sinless, she escapes the corruption (separation of body and soul, and decay of the body), that occurs after death and therefore enters immediately into glory.

The second truth that we are celebrating in Mary's Assumption is that this feast foreshadows our own destiny, or as the *Catechism of the Catholic Church* expresses it, an *"anticipation of the resurrection of other Christians."* St. Paul writes in his first letter to the Corinthians, *"if there is no resurrection of the dead, then Christ has not been raised; if Christ has not been raised, then our preaching is in vain and your faith is in vain" (1 Corinthians 15:13–14).* Indeed, Christ is risen from the dead! By contemplating Mary in glory, we are in a very real way contemplating our own destiny, which is resurrection. It is then obvious what Mary is doing, specifically through her Assumption: she is taking us out of ourselves and beyond ourselves.

The year 1950, when this dogma was proclaimed, was a time of great historical significance. The twentieth century was a time of unspeakable horror in which the sacredness of the human body and life was denied at every level. In the first half of the twentieth century, through ideologies such as Marxism and Nazism, the sacredness of the body was denied through the slaughter of millions in the gulags and concentration camps. In the second half of the twentieth century, this denial of the sacredness of the human body continued through the killing of untold millions through abortion and euthanasia. This horror, unfortunately, continues to this day.

Therefore, we can see in the timing of the proclamation of this dogma the workings of providence. It is important though to realize that Mary's Assumption is not merely a new idea that originated in the twentieth century. The reality of Mary's Assumption has been in the hearts and minds of Christians from the very beginning. There is nothing explicitly in the New Testament about Mary's Assumption for the simple reason that, most likely, much of the New Testament was written before this event occurred. However, the Assumption is one of those truths that was passed on by word of mouth directly from the Apostles.

Already in the fourth century in the East, Mary was implicitly honored in her Assumption by a celebration known as *The Memory of Mary*. The purpose of this celebration was to honor the "birthday" of Mary, that is, her entrance into heaven. *The Memory of Mary* was later renamed and became the feast of the *Dormitio*, or the "Falling asleep" of Mary. The *Dormitio* celebrated the death, resurrection, and Assumption of Mary and was celebrated widely by the fifth century. The Assumption enjoys a similarly ancient tradition in the West, so much so that even Protestant reformers acknowledged it. Martin Luther himself said, *"There can be no doubt that the Virgin Mary is in heaven. How this happened we do not know. . . . It is enough to know that she lives in Christ."*[38] Hence, the beauty and the truth of Mary's Assumption has been universally known and believed in by most Christians. What then could Mary be trying to communicate to us through her Assumption?

THE MESSAGE OF THE ASSUMPTION

The message of the Assumption is twofold. It reminds us of who we are and where we are going. St. John writes in his first letter in the New Testament,

> *See what love the Father has given us, that we should be called*
> *children of God; and so we are. . . . We are God's children now;*
> *it does not yet appear what we shall be, but we know that when*
> *he appears we shall be like him, for we shall see him as he is.*
> *—1 John 3:1–2*

Through Mary's Assumption we get a glimpse into this beautiful reality that St. John is describing. What is that reality? It is that we are children of God, and that we are moving toward this direct vision of God that is heaven. These two truths are what life is about, and nothing else.

Mysteriously, we almost never hear this message in our modern secular society. Rather, through the world of advertising, social media, and the mainstream media, we are often coerced to believe that our identity and destiny can be found here in this world. If you subscribe to a certain political persuasion and promote the right causes, many believe, then you are an important member of society because you are helping to push humanity forward. If one does not buy the version of life that the media tries to promote and instead subscribes to a more religious and transcendent view of life, one is often labeled a religious fanatic or an ultra-conservative.

The Christian world view, expressed vividly in Mary's Assumption, avoids any attachments and labels to anything of this world, not because the world is bad and not because certain causes are not worth fighting for, but ultimately because we are pilgrims passing through this life. For children of God, our only home is in heaven.

Throughout this whole book, I have attempted to illustrate that Mary's interior life is not only perfect but is also meant to be an icon or blueprint of what our own interior life is meant to look like. Specifically, by meditating on Mary's interior life, we see how we should act, what we should think, and who needs to be the center of our life. What is the fruit of such an interior life? We glimpse it in the Assumption of Mary. It is resurrection, the beatific vision, eternity with God.

Mary's life is our destiny. For us here in this world we are meant to live primarily by faith, hope, and love. Mary's presence is a reminder to us, a confident assurance, that what her Son has begun in our Baptism reaches its fulfillment in our own Passover from this life. It contains the hopeful reminder to us that death is not the end of life. Rather, death is really the beginning—of eternal life.

Throughout history, many people have spoken about God and about heaven. Mary, however, has the deepest experience and knowledge of what God and heaven are like. Regarding heaven St. Paul says, *"No eye has seen, nor ear heard, nor the heart of man conceived, what God has prepared for those who love him"* (*1 Corinthians 2:9*). These beautiful words of St. Paul are true with one exception: Mary sees and hears, and her heart knows what God has prepared for those who love him. Her life, certainly on earth, but now fully in heaven, radiates the fullness of the life of her Son Jesus. It is through her then that heaven becomes perceptible, and we can begin to glimpse that farther shore that is our destiny.

A FINAL MARIOLOGICAL POINT

I would like to conclude this book by highlighting an important Mariological point that can also serve as a summary for everything we have been reflecting on thus far. This point, I believe, cannot be stressed enough, because it provides the basic reasoning regarding the importance of Mary both for our spiritual life and our theological understanding. The point is this: we have no genuine understanding of Mary apart from the revelation of God in the Incarnation. Without the Incarnation Mary would never be known. But also, we do not have any experience and understanding of Jesus without Mary. Put simply, we do not have any understanding of Mary apart from Jesus and we do not have any understanding of Jesus without Mary. Therefore, St. Louis de Montfort concludes that *"Jesus is always and everywhere the fruit and Son of Mary, and Mary is everywhere the genuine tree that bears the fruit of life, the true Mother who bears the Son."*[39]

This is a truth that we witness in the Incarnation, since it is only through Mary that Jesus comes to us. Also, we witness this truth in our own spiritual lives, as we reflect on Jesus's words to St. John from the cross, *"Behold, your mother!"* *(John 19:27).* It is here now at the Assumption of Mary where we witness this truth eschatologically, since Mary is the first fruits of the Resurrection. Therefore, Mary is present in the beginning, in the middle, and in the end. What is she doing that entire time? She is taking us out of ourselves and beyond ourselves.

Mary begins by giving us God, a revelation so profound and earth-shattering that our hearts and minds transcend themselves in simply contemplating this revelation. Throughout our entire lives, specifically our lives of discipleship, Mary is forming us, guiding us, and teaching us how to live our lives in response to this revelation. Finally, in her Assumption, Mary reveals to us what is her glory, and by doing so, she reveals to us our destiny. Therefore, we can never underestimate the significance and the importance of Mary, nor should we ever worry about being too close to her.

Mary is, in essence, God's masterpiece. His masterpiece is not simply someone he keeps for himself to admire, but rather he shares her with each one of us. Mary is our mother, our sister, and our friend. She is our teacher, formator, and model of discipleship. She is holier than all the saints combined, and regardless of what we might think, her holiness does not make her distant from us and therefore out of reach. Rather, it is her holiness that draws her to us, who are still walking as pilgrims on this earth.

A good friend of mine who is a Carmelite cloistered nun once shared with me how difficult it was for her to develop a relationship with Mary. This nun grew up in a home where her mother was a perfectionist. Whenever her children did not do things perfectly she would become visibly angry and often yell and demean her children. This nun grew up terrified of ever making a mistake and spent most of her teenage years anxious, afraid, and hesitant to do anything because of how her mother might respond. As she began to study the Catholic faith more deeply, pray more regularly, and attend daily Mass in her early 20s, she said that the Church's teachings about Mary, specifically her Immaculate Conception and her Assumption, left this nun once again anxious and afraid. This was because she naturally projected onto Mary her earthly mother's perfectionist nature with all of its negative fruits.

Rather than run away from Mary, this nun would spend time each day praying and speaking to Mary from her heart and exposing to her all her fears and doubts regarding Mary's motherhood. One day, while she was alone in church, she was sitting before a statue of Mary and meditating on the Assumption. Suddenly, she says, she received the grace to realize that Mary was nothing like her earthly mother, because Mary's perfection, both in her birth and in her glory, were not weapons that Mary was using against her. Rather, they became a place of refuge where this nun could be loved, nurtured, and formed correctly, that is, with gentleness, patience, and love. Mary, she said, began to take her out of herself and beyond herself. May we allow Mary to do the same with us.

Notes

1 Code of Canon Law, 603.

2 Morning Offering prayer.

3 *The Liturgy of the Hours*, Vol. 1 (New York: Catholic Book Publishing Corp, 1975), 345-46).

4 Caryl Houselander, *The Reed of God: A New Edition of a Spiritual Classic* (Notre Dame, IN: Ave Maria Press, 2020), 68.

5 St. Louis de Montfort, *The Secret of Mary* (Bay Shore, NY: Montfort Publications, 1988, 2017), 269.

6 St. Louis de Montfort, *True Devotion to the Blessed Virgin* (Bay Shore, NY: Montfort Publications, 1988, 2017), 306.

7 Fr. Emil Neubert, *Life of Union with Mary*, Reprint Edn. (New Bedford, MA: Academy of the Immaculate, 2014), 90, 94.

8 St. Maximilian Kolbe, *Let Yourself Be Led by the Immaculate*, Kindle Edn. (St. Marys, KS, 2013), n.p.

9 Thomas Merton, *New Seeds of Contemplation* (New York: New Directions, 2007), 169.

10 Fulton Sheen, *The World's First Love* (San Francisco, Ignatius Press, 2011), 45.

11 Jean-Pierre De Caussade, *Abandonment to Divine Providence* (New York: Doubleday, 1975), 23.

12 *The Liturgy of the Hours*, Vol. III (New York: Catholic Book Publishing Corp, 1975), 1445.

13 A Monk, *The Hermitage Within* (Collegeville, MN: Cistercian Publications, 1977, 1999), 119.

14 St. Louis de Montfort, *The Secret of Mary*, 277.

15 Michael E. Gaitley, MIC, *33 Days to Morning Glory: A Do-It-Yourself Retreat In Preparation for Marian Consecration* (Stockbridge, MA: Marian Press, 2011).

16 Fr. Stefano Maria Manelli, *The Marian Vow* (New Bedford, MA: Academy of the Immaculate, 2010), 86-87.

17 Fulton Sheen, *The World's First Love*, 104.

18 St. Alphonsus Liguori, *The Glories of Mary* (Gastonia, NC: TAN Books, 1977, 2012), 413).

19 *The Collected Works of St. John of the Cross: The Ascent of Mount Carmel* (Washington, DC: Institute of Carmelite Studies, 1991),166.

20 St. Maximilian Kolbe, quoted in *Kolbe: Saint of the Immaculata*, ed. Br. Francis M. Kalvelage, FI (New Bedford, MA: Academy of the Immaculate, 2001), 178-179.

21 Francis Johnston, *The Wonder of Guadalupe* (Gastonia, NC: TAN books, 1993), n.p.

22 *The Liturgy of the Hours*, Vol. 1, 427.

23 *The Passion of the Christ*, directed by Mel Gibson (Santa Monica, CA: Icon Entertainment International, 2004).

24 *Mary in the Church: A Selection of Teaching Documents* (Washington, DC: United States Conference of Catholic Bishops, 2003), 65.

25 St. John Paul II, *Rosarium Virginis Marie* #13.

26 *Mary the Mother of God: Sermons by St. Gregory Palamas* (Dalton, PA: Mount Thabor Publishing, 2005), 36.

27 Columba Marmion, *Christ the Life of the Soul* (Chestnut Ridge, NY: B. Herder Book Company, 1922), 414.

28 Venerable Mary of Agreda, *The Mystical City of God* (Gastonia, NC: TAN books, 1978), 50.

29 St. Louis de Montfort, *True Devotion to the Blessed Virgin*, 298.

30 *The Writings of St. Maximilian Maria Kolbe*, Vol. II: Various Writings, (Florence, Italy: Nerbini International, 2022), 2244.

31 *The Collected Works of St. John of the Cross: The Ascent of Mount Carmel*, 362.

32 St. Alphonsus Liguori, *The Glories of Mary*, 28.

33 Fr. Emile Nuebert, *Life of Union with Mary*, 5-6.

34 Msgr. Romano Guardini, *The Rosary of Our Lady* (Nashua, NH: Sophia Institute Press, 1998), 58.

35 St. John Paul II, *Rosarium Virginis Marie*, 16.

36 *The Writings of St. Maximilian Maria Kolbe*, Vol. II: Various Writings, 2105.

37 Edward Sri, *Queen Mother: A Biblical Theology of Mary's Queenship* (Steubenville, OH: Emmaus Road Publishing, 2005), 14.

38 *Mariology: A Guide for Priests, Deacons, Seminarians, and Consecrated Persons*, Seat of Wisdom Books (Goleta, CA: Queenship Publishing, 2007), 337.

39 St. Louis de Montfort, *True Devotion to the Blessed Virgin*, 301.

ABOUT PARACLETE PRESS

PARACLETE PRESS IS THE PUBLISHING ARM of the Cape Cod Benedictine community, the Community of Jesus. Presenting a full expression of Christian belief and practice, we reflect the ecumenical charism of the Community and its dedication to sacred music, the fine arts, and the written word.

SCAN
TO
READ

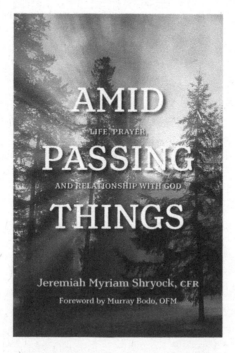